CANTILENA

Also by John Peck

Shagbark (Bobbs-Merrill, New York,1972)
The Broken Blockhouse Wall (David R. Godine, Boston, 1979)
Poems and Translations of Hī-Lö (Carcanet Press, Manchester, 1991, & Sheep Meadow Press, Riverdale-on-Hudson, NY, 1993)
Argura (Carcanet Press, Manchester, 1993)
Selva Morale (Carcanet Press, Manchester, 1995)
M and Other Poems (Triquarterly Books, Evanston, IL, 1996)
Collected Shorter Poems 1966–1996 (Carcanet Press, Manchester, 1999, & Triquarterly Books, Evanston, IL, 2003)
Red Strawberry Leaf: Selected Poems 1994–2001 (University of Chicago Press, Chicago, 2005)
Contradance (University of Chicago Press, Chicago, 2011)
I Came, I Saw – Eight Poems (Shearsman Books, Bristol, 2012)

Translations

Euripides: *Orestes* (with Frank Nisetich, Oxford University Press, New York / Oxford, 1995)
C.G. Jung: *Liber Novus / The Red Book* (with Sonu Shamdasani and Mark Kyburz, W.W. Norton & Co., New York / London, and the Philemon Foundation, 2009.)

John Peck

CANTILENA

one book in four spans

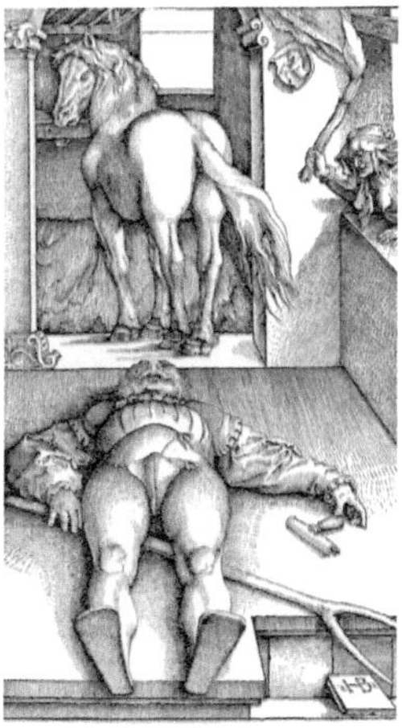

Shearsman Books

Published in the United Kingdom in 2016 by
Shearsman Books Ltd
50 Westons Hill Drive
Emersons Green
BRISTOL
BS16 7DF

www.shearsman.com

ISBN 978-1-84861-473-4

ACKNOWLEDGMENTS

With my gratitude to the following for first publishing certain cantos:

Herbert Golder, *Arion* (ser. 3/6.2, 1998): *Denarius* #37, adapted from '*Corpus nostrum*';

Alex Houen and Adam Piette, *Blackbox Manifold* (#9, 2012): *Denarius* #s 1-4;

John Matthias, *Notre Dame Review* (# 39, 2014, & #20, 2005): *Cedars of Liban* #s 49-57, and *Denarius* #31, as 'Here' (in tribute to the sculpture of Emily Young);

From my own *Inizia* (Rhino Editions, Magnolia, MA 2001): *Caelum* #64 incorporates part of 'Twenty-One-Dowel Garden Rake,' and the title poem is modified in *The Bewitched Groom* #1;

Michael Schmidt, *PN Review* (PNR 296, 2012): *Cedars of Liban* #s 35-44, and *PNR* 177, 2007: *The Bewitched Groom* #12 in a prior version;

———, ed., *Five American Poets.* Carcanet Press, Manchester, 2010, Foreword by Clive Wilmer: *Caelum* #s 20-22, adapted from 'Random-bench';

Reginald Shepherd, *Bayou* (#45, 2005): *The Bewitched Groom* #8, adapted from 'Martyrdom of Peter';

Sarah Spence, *Literary Imagination* (4.I, 2002): *The Bewitched Groom* #s 61, 62, adapted from 'Ogdoad';

Jon Thompson, *Free Verse: A Journal of Poetry and Poetics*, issue 25, Summer 2014: *Cedars of Liban* #s 31-33, 41-43, 65, 67;

Arto Vaun, *Locomotive* (I.1, Fall/Winter 2015): *Denarius* #s 17, 18.

To early readers, particular thanks: Reginald Gibbons, John Gittins, Elizabeth T. Gray, Jr., Jock Ireland, Nate Klug, John Matthias, Joan Gowett Peck, Rosanna Warren, Wallis Wilde-Menozzi, Clive Wilmer.

The images on the title page are a votive hand of Hermes, bronze, Rome, 2nd C, (Louvre Museum, Paris), drawing by author, and a wood engraving by Hans Baldung Grien, 'Der behexte Stallknecht' [The Bewitched Groom], ca. 1544.

CANTILENA

In the Designer are all the cogwheels that control the movements of the Harrow, and this machinery is regulated according to the inscription demanded by the sentence… Of course the script can't be a simple one; it's not supposed to kill a man straight off, but only after an interval of, on an average, twelve hours… When it finishes the first draft of the inscription on the man's back, the layer of cotton wool begins to roll and slowly turns the body over, to give the Harrow fresh space for writing… It keeps on writing deeper and deeper for the whole twelve hours… How quiet he grows at just about the sixth hour! Enlightenment comes to the most dull-witted. It begins around the eyes. From there it radiates. A moment that might tempt one to get under the Harrow itself. Nothing more happens than that the man begins to understand the inscription, he purses his mouth as if he were listening. You have seen how difficult it is to decipher the script with one's eyes; but our man deciphers it with his wounds.

—Franz Kafka, 'In der Strafkolonie,'
translated by Willa and Edwin Muir

Nabat!

— 'The Alarm Bell'
(4th movement, 11th Symphony, Dmitri Shostakovich)

Falling In
—A Foreword to John Peck's *Cantilena*—

1.

John Peck relates a story about the artist James Turrell, innovator of 'inner-light' installations and the massive, decades-long desert observatory project at Arizona's Roden Crater. During one of Turrell's museum shows, two visitors to the darkened rooms mistook the projected corner-cube of blue light for a reliably solid wall, leaned on it, and promptly fell inside the piece. While such an experience may sound intriguing to those of us frustrated by material form's inadequacy in the face of experience, the visitors were not amused. Each filed a lawsuit against the artist.

Under-read, underrated, and without the mainstream attention focused on Turrell, John Peck need not fear legal retribution for the risks posed by his long poem, *Cantilena.* However, Peck's magnum opus, a serial work in the recent tradition of Geoffrey Hill and Jay Wright, and harkening back to the medieval sequences of Remy de Gourmont, contains the same surface enchantments, animating vitalities, and fathomless depths that surely bewitched the Turrell gazers. "Now that I have let it go, / it can touch me—the many gone, / their ozone margin of departure." *Cantilena* is a poem about falling in, and learning to fall in deeper.

Peck's poem is divided into four books, or "spans," each with an appended motto. The paradoxical and physical bent to each of these mottoes ("sluicing roots," "squaring circles") gives the reader some idea of what she's in for. While each motto strikes a keynote in one span, it also resounds in others. "In the domain / of the small, just this side of doing, / the percolation of focus / refuses to resolve even as it meshes / here, there, and there," as Peck writes in span two. Announced but unscheduled, these pointers gently keep one's footing on alert.

Plunging into equivocations with Peck's personal ghosts, above all his father Clarence (whose engineering work in the heat-treatment of steel alloys contributed secretly to the Manhattan Project), the book also falls into a sustained, skeptical dialogue with the "familiar compound ghosts" of Western culture. Shostakovich, Marsden Hartley, Thoreau,

Karl Barth, Oscar Milosz—these are names culled from the poem's first fifteen cantos. "It becomes clear / that my thoughts have not been mine, ever," Peck writes. But this echo of Jung's *Red Book* amounts to more than an acknowledgment of intellectual indebtedness. An unpublished essay by Peck on aspects of the poem notes the harmonic between this perpetual in-falling and the notes struck in both German and English usage.

> When one asks, "Can you think of anything we can do?" it runs, *Fällt uns etwas ein, was wir tun könnten?* The English phrasing is naively activist where the German allows for the fact that in-fall happens: *Einfallen* signals the psychological facts straightaway, the *Einfall* being a strange notion or lucky hunch, but also the routine occurrence of thinking. The Wintersian critique of radical associationism in poetics, although now mostly ignored, remains indispensable. Yet so also does the Aristotelian account of root breath ψυκέ (*anima* and *soul*), as the pooled potentials of "inner touch" that ground sensing and phantasy alike. Neurology goes on revamping this account without entirely junking it. And so in English, *it occurs* to me—that is, runs in front of me, crosses my path; or else it strikes me, that is, hits, grazes, grooves into, or rubs up against me, because 'I' am the field into which *it* falls; such is the common reality of experience.

One of the great pleasures of *Cantilena* is feeling this reality ramify in a way that, for all the poem's learnedness, is primarily physical. Fleshed out in contours of syntax and bursts of raw lyricism, Peck's verse is precise even when abstract: "judgment / remanding life to convicted wonder."

2.

Thematically, *Cantilena* appropriates subjects familiar to the Modernist long poem: recent European and American history, art making, political corruption and the question of individual complicity, and the bearing of classical and religious heritages on the present. *Cantilena* is also one of our only major long poems so far to consistently engage climate change. Yet, for this reader at least, the work's chief power comes not from the positions it stakes out on these topics, but rather from its performance of a kind of imaginative magic—what Peck calls "undersensing." This "undersensing" is carried out in three distinct arenas: historical vignettes, personal remembrances, and synchronicities snatched from a lifetime of reading. It is no exaggeration to say that the poem treats the dead, in Henry Vaughan's words, as "alive and busie." These stand-offs with ghosts inform the flux of the speaker's self, often caught between curiosity and terror: "Though they only stand there, they came many miles, / and though you wait, you'll be the first to move."

Each of the four books or "spans" proceeds, in High Modernist fashion, by juxtaposition. The speaker's archetypal vision of lightning sheathing a tower—"the windows blown out / but mortar holding its shaking length"—jumps to an anecdote of the 16th-century goldsmith Benvenuto Cellini as a child, witnessing a salamander "cavorting / in the core-blue coals." A canto beginning with Herakles and Alkestis, "veiled in toile," transforms by the end into a lament for a World Trade Center survivor, her "muteness" wrapped in a "grit stole." As in dreamwork or a Poundian ideogram, meaning is to be stumbled upon and must be pieced together.

The word "undersense" comes from Wordsworth's *Prelude,* and Peck infuses it with heavy doses of his own idiosyncratic gnosticism and Renaissance alchemy (books two and three of the poem take their titles from this field). Poetry becomes a way of feeling through, feeling beneath. When Peck writes about a Pittsburgh lecture hall in which both he and his father spoke, forty years apart, or about a New England landscape still vibrant with the Shakers' "regimental / abandon," this "undersensing" alters our relationship with the past, or, better yet, newly reveals it. "The crack thus worked open pours out what is." Watching these cracks emerge throughout the poem is often thrilling, and yet the charge is inescapably moral. "Depth comes over us, and in it we look up." Peck's reading of a late Thom Gunn poem, 'A Wood Near Athens,' could apply equally to his own work in *Cantilena*. "Depth burns all the way around suffering and causal thinking, for visionary powers do not stitch events together, but make them transparent to whole light." Imagine a pair of lenses, like movie glasses, that allow you to perceive history along with still emerging reality in 3-D, with all five senses, its horrors and joys arising from the sidewalk you stand on, the air you breathe.

If *Cantilena* is often about this paradoxical plunge into alertness, "falling as being pulled, / dragged as breaking surface and gulping flame," it also demands that readers plunge into it, undaunted. As with Hill and Wright (and the master who stands behind all three poets, Ezra Pound), Peck's combination of linguistic density and historical allusions proves demanding. Such is the wager for what Peck calls "the potentials of sensing with the whole organism." And just as one lovely turn in the poem remarks on a "foretime of the eye before it judges," so too does our apprehension of *Cantilena* come in stages. The poem's first canto acknowledges those "fit disturbers whom the mind loathes / yet down through its girderwork / of unrealized ends may crave." From this inaugural disturbance—which may also represent the moment of poetic vocation—to a constant jostling between loathing and craving, political dirge and lyric rapture, *Cantilena* enacts discoveries of its own of mood and tone. "Follow the clue patiently and you will understand nothing," avows Basil Bunting, another abiding influence on Peck, towards the end of his long poem, *Briggflatts*.

If the speaker/traveler in *Cantilena* had plotted out his route beforehand, he would forego the poem's principle of receptivity, its acknowledgment of language's strange but compelling mutuality: "salmon after their stream climb / in a deep eddy holding, / stippled missiles / long as an arm: I carry my load / and if I bear it then it will carry me." One wonders, at times, how the poem ever came to a stop. Yet in fact Peck does halt it—restarting the poem with its last and longest span, *The Bewitched Groom*, by addressing a goddess of beginnings on a beach at low tide:

> Inizia—
> withholdings, curses, all their damnable protest
> under my breath seeking some absconder
> *Hell!* bits of smooth glass in the shatterfield
> of the beach splayed wide by ebb,
> choice marzipan spat out by process,
> gleaming in your allowing
> ease: no further, no deeper need I burrow
> to find your donation.
>   All resistance slides
> in runnels out to the shine, placid seepings
> of release.

Zero disc in the wind rolling
hints of itself, the key ring at your girdle
hourly undoing prisoners' bindings
and ting-tings through the running lights of a freighter
in the bay's roadstead, miles out into a patience
assured of the wharf's hug and unloading.
Never
late the meeting—punctual even down
the corridor of crime, as the ripe pear confides,
as the shower flouncing from cloud swag announces,
On time :
my hand is the work of millennia
and thus too its work, yet in thanks becomes only what,
lifting and valving into the unmeasured,
I give you, rebeginner of grasps and pourings.

You visited? You abandoned? You are always here.

This *I*, jostled by Jung's Wotanic "disturbers" in the poem's first canto, returns here as devotee, able to let things fall out in due time.

3.

Jung in Pittsburgh, Hölderlin in West Hartford, Mandelstam in Princeton at midnight: Peck's poem leaves no shortage of compound ghosts to tantalize us. Likewise, depth psychology (after leaving academia, Peck has practiced Jungian analysis since 1993), Native American mythology, and Hindu theology all provide points of entry to the poem. One crucial canto even has a soccer referee undergo a Poundian metamorphosis into a player (perhaps a stand-in for the writer himself becoming a helpless participant): "No wonder that no side wants him on their team." But for a poem so invested in performing and revealing what it senses, physicality remains crucial. Even at his most discursive, Peck always prioritizes sound. His teacher Donald Davie once wrote that poetry's job was to turn ideas into sensation; in *Cantilena* language snaps and shifts, involving the reader in its "singly entranced yet mutually / entangled" predicament.

In that respect, the poem's comprehensive *Einfall* is the sounding of its discourse.

One of Peck's early poems, 'Vestibule,' describes a husband and wife calling to each other from different floors of a house. For the man, the woman's voice conjures up "another room we entered once together, / Catching our breath": the room for self-recollection used by Shakers for spiritual preparation after fieldwork. Longing resolves itself, this early poem suggests, not in direct communication, but in patches of peace granted by cultural inheritance and mutual curiosity. Likewise, for all its recondite and unflinching excavation, *Cantilena* feels its way towards the same momentary resolutions. "As a hull enters / a berg's wake or a whale's, that spreading calm / after large passage, / its muted draw silkenly forgiving / micro-seethings across the dark total. / One follows." One falls in, deeper and deeper in this remarkable work, to see what's really there.

Nate Klug

One

CEDARS OF LIBAN

sluicing roots

1

My paper-covered half-pillar
near the door to hold letters, in shutter-louvred
storm light sinks deeper away, as if
to retreat from that not-yet tipped
beaker where powers fizz, eldest primes,
fit disturbers whom the mind loathes
yet down through its girderwork
of unrealized ends may crave. Thus taking these in
I give *I* no assent. The bear
through valleys of my ancestors, crooner
to the loners, hulked as the slant warbler
of trailbreak, a furry sun ululant—
as Odin, cloud on cloud
fertile and urgent, hung on
the tree nine days and nights, until from his sweat
the oozing runes jelled and roots knuckled
tumescent toward the showering undersky
of earth's want: unaccountable
helmsman, gang-builder out of black cumulus,
tuner of cedars and sirocco
and the oak architraves of the Teutoburg,
who littered the Kalkriese
with Latin iron and fertilizing bone—
again you are here, all unsent for.

2

Not from Pleiku but Sumer's garden
where through millennia arbors extend the house
blossom by blade into space, for a fifth year
unstoppably piled the uncounted. Melville, Higginson,
Duyckinck, Emerson: how should one imagine
briefing them, movers of Young America, Mazzini
and Słowacki's cousins, on these redcoat wars?
Orchards from origin, each tree a willed effort—from
their years of smash one glimpse here makes selvage.
In front of Marsden Hartley's *Mount Ktaadn*
a twelve-year-old surrenders her arms at her sides,
filaments siphoning the unseen
at intermission from the out-takes of death.
The bulk dark of it shoulders fires into space
neither as spangle nor aura but the bloom of itself.
Her lips part: she does not hear them pounding,
strewing their beachheads, the great simplifiers.
The mineral ages are only as wide as she is, they are going
on into her, who will thrust yowls from her belly
and cup leaf-pale hands in a hospice.
Nothing can stop this, nothing makes any of it
either plunge on or hold back. Going in or rising,
going on in or lifting out of it: mountain, sun.

3

Dressage!—a red-brown door bulges and rips
the sun's torpid delay, then muzzle and foreleg,
roan kick and a mane percolating
through fence and hill, a cloud cliff sheared
by sternum and belly: Poussin's mount and rider
sprung from their barn are the least of it. Wiry
glory half blurry, fascists spurring the wishists,
twinging knot of the two ways. How do we stand it?
There it goes—assertion leaping past argument,
lungs sucking a hot chaw of teeth, seeing caught
at the boil, raw fight afloat there
past policy, out-churning advance.
Yet at stand, at bend, sagged from shoulders
slotting down the neck's fringey pour, breakout
mauls grass all at maze, archived with oats,
bone sheathing the fat of the wind now, blood hairy,
the eye a black pin through plush.
No innocent, the soul broods in dunged hayey
dolor past nightfall, hurls men its enemies at the horizon,
sublimes its contract past praise into stamina: *Love evil!*
Clatters toward cumulus and trots back
trailing a dust cloud of the dead
baptized but clamoring, their omertà
trembling the window wall in nude daylight.

4

My station café early, the same faces,
but the threads run back now to their points of departure,
tug on this one for love:
there sat the defeated successful man,
through the Aarau tunnel at dawn
from the branch line where Barth labored on Romans—
the Nazibahn. His table a flotation device,
publicly private, his thread trailing from some gray lake
whose glow seeped, pearl against pall,
from sadness an improbable, possible bliss.
The acetylene of young Barth's Paul had burrowed in,
the whole cosmos groans to be set free, loosed from miasmas,
to take on glory as we are destined, beyond our pain, to know glory.
The glazed full thing hung there, gray over pearl,
my illuminated solid. There, weird away.
Cold mist. And mist smell. Paul's vision was not my vision,
but it had been. Paul's version
accelerates the whole, as hummingly
as a big electric
retreats free of load,
warm from its run, picking up speed
while still in the Bahnhof, past strings
of cars being made up, past window cliffs
as massively as those tons shoot keening into the blaze.

5

Caustic, both-ways Thoreau sauntered into the word-glade
after his lost hound, horse, and dove, returning
as the lone drinker. And then he got down
on his tummy to watch the queen ant
lift from her city's vent
and rose to bless Brown's bowie knife at the lecture,
that steel thence to Kanzas. What's with this bachelor katabasis,
this Underground Man? Holed up in Ar-kansas
the Titan-II crews chew on dry rations
but now the repair team drops a wrench three stories
through the fuel tank. Green cloud over klaxons, that was Damascus.
To be down in it with the thing it is not, together,
the migrant thing it is meant to become: being many is singular,
while singling out the way is manifold.
Singling the way out, though: that is the masterpiece.
Only those moves that are necessary, and only
by staying with them did they find their way back,
not three critters but ten men in gas masks. Yet in the first act a rifle
hangs above the fireplace. No one mentions it. It will speak.
I tell my gang down there,
take no phantasm plainly. Turn over
the upended bug, suck on your siloed almond.
Hermes has stranded us in our loud kitchen.
Off it goes, six-legged and with feelers for eyes.

6

Ferragosto vacuums the centro storico
to a stage set across which huge Fellini
in morose hurry zigs by and squeezes
into a telephone booth. That glimpse stands
memento mori now, the calls Collect, accepted.
Yin in the bedrock ideograms
is reed-shaded zero for a crane's brood
on the north banks of rivers, south-facing slopes.
Or the hut for a kid king hard on his father's death.
But prodigal? I abandoned in another country
all the handholds other men would have held fast.
Heat-ripple climbed the open window
over an alley aimed at Via del Governo Vecchio,
warren of the vanished bureaucracy.
Rome narrowed to that five-story slice
through unpeopled August
melting the frame's sunny null. Between then and now
streams now, reeds tower through vacancy,
shark sheen rotting the foot of each swaying flute
though the pot I shattered gave space back to space.
On the ledge, one bowl, ample enough
to rinse a newborn. Old yin stands as nursery
for a bawling, dripping alloy
stringy, pink, laced with strontium,...

7

...which inaugurates a continuing cry:
phantasia was his restrained category
for the thunderclap that he alone heard
in his tent, or mounted, or on foot: Marcus, emperor.
Followed by an outcry, then assent.
The trick: one must decline to populate the outcry.
Below my baked ledge, motorbikes rev then fade.
Yet the potter swopped up scorched oxide, his pigment,
and, with the arrogance of Apelles,
swirled a blue overlapping
on the inner crown of my brown crock.
Death my neighbor has staffed his cornice
with a breasty messenger, puckery receptionist,
leaving her complexion to rot and grow
fruitful, scaling without falling.
And so a shameless overplus curls
out of noon darkly bisqueing the stone sill,
the table setting, south-facing wall past the window,
this lap of the labyrinthine rampart,
and I have not counted the hours, for shall increments
accuse the continuous hand of the heaper?
And I let move my mind's motion
in a signing spiral around the finely
gritty brain pan of the baked water clock.

8

The Prodigal shipped out in Melville's 1840s,
a bloated leg on Tai Pi already signifying
satiated longing, lands in fee simple,
no contentions over inheritance
from the father, green life itself the grantor.
Fenimore Cooper, *Henry* Thoreau, *Tawney* Melville—
a South Marquesan penchant for renaming
anchored my upstart priors,
peregrine *Tawney* postdating himself savage
and negro. Son-in-law to Chief Justice Shaw,
he dedicated Typee's *entertainment*
to that magistrate of counting house and mill race
and rail head expansion. In my study hangs
a saber, from an engineer's battalion,
its hilt-cup volute 18th-century. They were stationed
on Bataan, weeks from Melville's layover, two empires
grinding their expansions through each other,
its owner on home-front assignment and so not witness
to his own men going down under the breadfruit,
that elm-grove cousin in Tawney's book, lush mulberry
like him vagrant from tradition. The blade's etching,
Clarence Peck, 1927, silvery,
eighty-five years in the trees between us, cools
the light, loading the branches, pebbly grenades.

9

The invitation was for us to stay over,
Hugh Kenner and the nurse-wife
who had saved him, our child and their children
bouncing on waterbeds while *The Knower*
spoke sentences as pointedly composed of particulars
as Fuller's flexy sticks
and knobs in primary colors
combobulating on his desk and floating
above it—*The Pound Era* their similar
bulked open, not a stale right angle in sight:
thus *Utna-pishtim* in his Bucky-chair
tilting back, *Mr. Faraway*, me leaning forward
situated inches from recital:
the first 150 lines of *The Dunciad*
from memory in his pinched semi-lisp,
all this before double-checking invocations
of the moon god, the route past Mount Mashu,
and scorpion sentinels on the sun's road.
Because his father had taught Latin, or because
Pound knew better than to deny
a soaking, Kenner survived the flood.
From Faraway the Knower I learned that one could lace Bucky-sticks
into a hull twenty cubits on a side.
And went down, almost, to the ship.

10

Learning, past the thumbed index,
holding my tongue through lulls in the kitchen
with the women, between laid crust
and poured filling—being, that is, no doctor of bees
weaving through his gored Africa, ears alive
for their cologned signals. Nor Melville fronting sea wind
with Consul Hawthorne in the dunes at Southport,
cigars brighter in the blown desolation, their warmth shearing
through the old talk, the sailor rekindling it
toward Egypt, Palestine, the silk of generations
tattering over tar smell in gale-force Providence,
salt everywhere along its grit-strewn carry, the scent
of strange cold fire. Deadpan ironizes skillet-banging, and belief
off-shores the actual task. Whereas kitchens bake things:
every 75 years, notes Bob Moses, *the constitutional people*
lurch forward against the counter-lurchers.
I had to: I could not live in this country unless I could change it.
And so a domestic breviary becomes possible:
the formula no longer is to portage hymns
or confess power's limitless presence. The pattern at ground
is the shower of fire from the fine
jangling in the speech-cloud
at length ripped asunder, where origin
dines on origin.

11

Bolt-erect, covers thrown—coughing in moonlight,
its rumpled path brighting knees mid-October,
comédie solitaire hocking itself
from the throat's loft, a missioning pendentive
smashing tablets to scatter Law down the mountain—
while peripherally one branch
which had lost twenty orange leaves that day
performs a Caesarian on our white sister.
And while, also, basso:
You say enough so that we know it is y o u *speaking*
but not enough to know w h a t *it is you are saying*—
the quid, not the pro quo,
with trailing stem sweeping to ground.
And you summoners? Fabulous-factual, *mortis* quick
then receding, you split across
the equal sign—no
testimonies from Garabandal, where showings
galvanized girls to run backwards at dusk
unharmed among sharp stones, their heads cocked skyward
at nothing among the peaks. Fifty years past them
peripherally at daybreak a van,
its tail a carbuncle, slithers backward
as the agent with a wrist-flick to the mound
heaves the socked cartridge of *The Times*.

12

An unmarked road in Nevada blurs into
Area 51, which does not exist
officially. Advisements theorize like Longinus:
BEYOND THIS POINT ANYTHING CAN HAPPEN
I have not seen it, could not see it if I reached it,
nor, if reaching it, subject it to amendment—my indentured shame
through zero-degree black humor
in belonging to this time: *the intense inane*
which Winters, who knew the desert, discerned
in the chimerae of our poetry
trembling above the line. Our little family
down an axle-breaker to Anasazi ruins
was stopped by one, two, three ravens: we were,
I am, the clueless thief
sweeping pantry shelves, his racket
swelling the pulse's infinitesimals,
drums backed against the wall—yet where surf
creams the axle sound of Parmeneides
and sinks hissing down streaky shine, a boy
kneels gaming with pebbles, their gurgle glare
streaming my girl's face and all that stays done,
Faust's poodle pulsing down the beach, going, gone,
the others not far. And closed, the wound in the air.

13

Thirteen designates protection—
no cloak of invisibility, and something
more than simply ducking bad luck. It splices
earthquake orders of meaning:
Old and New Covenants, Iudas and Matthias.
As the unity of twelve, it promotes death as godfather
to a thirteenth child: out there past the edge
of the natural logarithmic base—
so, either that child becomes a leader
or must die. Thus found the obit from Milton Shaw,
project chief on the *Nautilus*, Rickover's A-sub,
on the thirteenth anniversary of Father's death.
Whose sub reactor sheath trailed his work on the Project:
he, spared out from Bataan, Guadalcanal,
for the Bomb sheath which he must have wanted
in vengeance for his gone battalion, later
gave the fig to the Westinghouse brass when they said
they wanted him with them, upstairs—
so, from obscurity, through the Wirtschaftswunder,
onto a siding, he led himself home to himself,
officer-protector separated out,
manager-protector self-islanded, the terms for that
gummy in wash trailing from his time into
blue glare, an oar bouncing on his shoulder inland.

14

Duality in nature, duality in spirit, these
command even when easing back on their pressures.
How slow to acknowledge it: one must stay
caught in that pincer movement like some willing
quarry for Patton-Heraclitus, or else
duck the only fight worth the game.
Marie Curie observed her closed eye sponsoring
luminosities with radium salts at hand,
mere years before Jung watched sun seeping blood into
cavern torrents, eyes shock-shut in his study.
And Pierre Curie's scale for variable
magnetic charges tugging at metals and crystals,
climbing with heat, past 2,500 Fahrenheit
became within two decades Father's métier
of the marrying alloys, the swarming congeals. Pierre Curie
was struck on the rainy Pont Neuf by a wagon
lugging 6-plus tons of gear for the infantry.
His head, in the last seconds—the red flesh from halos
of the blast zone or in the bodies and fire ribbons
streaming from her chair, Holy Wisdom—
geysering into the Zone of Alienation,
lynx, wolf, and raptor sliding in edgewise,
eyelash and whisker into the inscrutable.

15

At 3 a.m. near Place Saint Sulpice, it was Oscar Milosz
womanly man, manly woman at the desk
by my hotel window onto a weedy courtyard,
asking me to inscribe his register—
he insisted, or she did, that we had spoken years earlier.
But when I bent forward, rainy lamplit glass
stopped me, fountain past sight in the square
trickling its capillary spread. His eyes, her light,
sank through the grain of all things, from blood and a brain
at the League of Nations for infant Lithuania,
gone by '39, before Fletcher Prouty
heard Winston musing the night Rotterdam went up:
Time and the ocean and some guiding star
and high cabal have made us what we are
to the tune of *Lili Marleen*. In that room,
blood was self-division—the panic sadness of aeons
one centimeter distant yet squirming inside,
whispering ease to death while gushing recollection—
not through the shock of false infinities
but the speed of place at a steady boil, our day as Turba
and putrefaction. And that has ballasted me
against what Myles Horton learned from drifters in the '30s:
If you grab onto a train going faster than you are,
it will swing you around, your legs flopping out
and knocking your grip loose, sending you under the wheels.

16

Misty tent-tops patch lawn as spidertown,
claimants from under, architects from axis,
yarners from Spindle City, who come back
with the same blueprint when brushed away.
Yet here, morning knowledge: in three hours
heat will sublime away the evidence,
making the figleaf oligarchies
indistinguishable from the soft
dictatorships, even the aristocracies
of perception from the democracies of death.
Young evening knowledge lounges abroad at noon
picking his teeth.... Unlike Ruskin, one cannot
assume that Plato's *Critias* gives us his broken-off
last word—all the gods of the universe on greed
or power-lust in the self-proclaimed heirs
to the moment. Nor revive
his smack-down of boostered Venetian Gothic.
Nor press Venice back into the groves
misty in Lebanon, this time rearing from
some up-to-the-armpits lagoon.
Every laurel shattered and blown by the marbled
pork loin of grab blesses fuse and rammed plunger
drifting crowns onto the oncoming.

17

Seventeen brands conquest. In the boasts
of those with Latin names
the count begins rattling *Veni, vidi*—therefore
Shostakovich was halted by
the winds and a hidden river from writing
a sixteenth symphony
and a trophy seventeenth, *vinci.*
Catch them swerving into hobo sensing,
dangling their ankles in side eddies,
those of the flowing way—
losers, stowing a compass, unwilling to teach
the winners how that erect pin
on which the iron canters at noon
wells from the shadowless where, for a wink, sagacity
lends no tarpaulin, its dark swallowed,
blood root mineral chilled.
The hired man in Frost's *Death of a Hired Man*
looked up Stafford at the Library of Congress—
et resurrexit—the blue heron from his marsh
digesting his own stanzas. Beyond
victory, beyond even gift, surges morning
that comes to me not again, but as raw novum
casting no shadows as it breathes me in.

18

In the Teutoburg, wild boars click the Geigers
cruising head-down, tap dancing Chernobyl
after three decades. I can assign them
to neither Arminius nor Varus, for they scuttle
dispatched by our own agency
against our own incapacity. Just who, bookkeepers
bent on your high stools, goes co-adjutant
with those legions strung out and hacked at for ten miles?
Liban's groves, not seen, not touched, go tick-tick
stilting on the legs of pachyderms
up through shade sway and faint surf, persistent
even though pillaged. Their half-life stiffs the calculus
and shines with specters, to my closed eyes as definite
as an Old Master, but unframed:
northern ocean and unsetting sun stuccoing
the sky with honey, a citadel's baroque
cupola pinning its port city. Turner's
early precision. Masts. Indecipherable ache
yet no French horns, minutes as days
in the swollen outlay. A question breaches,
unanswered, unanswerable
unless itself be the answer. And I want
nothing this place ever made, sheltered, or named,
surplus memorious, hoard and haven.

19

I want evil! yelled Jung at his great turn,
and when his devil appeared it became his joy—
not that his hells did not sting much and long,
but that the chasm stretches:
beyond even race murder, the Big Heat—
two hundred years into takeoff, yet still we deny
that oncoming evil comes from us. Even killers
fling from the rim of the canyon whole-body!
Which I can't, or won't, so—what I see
are the gulf's rippled thermals. Watery cliffs.
Fontana di Trevi half-sun and half-shadow
paved with coin tosses shimmying the wish
to have it both ways? There is no poetics without ethos,
no alley wall fountain
that does not babble forgiveness or annihilation
because I seek it, trembling
replenished. That water goes nowhere
and does everything—at hand, the ages, knee-deep
then past the waist a basin
may it slope on out, there
total compression
morally beyond.
But not to have stopped ourselves from not acting,
self-refutingly numb in the flow? Look at this too and pass on.

20

Your remnants and look-alikes and coffins of yourselves
have stopped me, *cedrus libani*—
an unhitched flatbed trailer in Times Square,
thirty-foot timbers from an excavation, two feet on a side,
the wear of two centuries a mud stain
near **MARINE RECRUITMENT** and spreading silence
as I stared at them—no one else
looking. Therefore, mute worthies, Saluti,
although your groves be legend, your carry warpless
through muck and sewage lies out in the day.
The unit, the monument, the site
corrode in rain while panels of your sheen
still redden crêches of force, lucre, louche ease,
dry storage, dry worship.
Herms tough on the gateways
there may not be, but glass, sheet steel, polymers
and bulk remember the plunges between your flanks.
Porting a scam casket through Midtown, black
muslin slipping, and skipping to keep step,
I went the stage of the processions, its grease paint and dust,
candles swaying against Rome's plague, torches
streaking Paris, the bombed Haymarket.
Here, cops and eight-story telescreens, but then
your whisper, *You are alive!*

21

Utu, chisels the Sumerian
tablet for old Bilgamesh*: the domain
of Utu is Cedar Mountain. Once the end
grows more definite, even in a land
amnesiac, fountaining mind
self-stoppered shakes itself for fizz
hankering to leave a monument
wedged among trunks thrusting from mold into
morning mist. Utu, he knows.
Utu Roi, crowned with Apollinaire's bandage.
Knows this cone-studded fir, tapering eighty
January feet? Into
brevetting sun, bemedaled. One looks up to rank,
but foggy now my date of enlistment.
The main thing is to snap straight, heave to,
but where do orders aim
if not here? arthritic rootlets veining
back up through grit, their pulse stationary.
The dripping understory times
not the enameled traffic blur but a newly
unsheathed claw of penthos
dripping katabasis
where I spin, rut creamed by my clowning wheels. Go
to the place where you can hear things. Stand still.

* Gilgamesh (*Izdubar* and *Bilgamesh* antedated Gilgamesh).

22

Sentiment corrodes the fathers,
Jefferson's rotunda rain-stained.
Daughters suffer more
from this attrition—keen-hearted earlier,
they look to dad's unhesitating preferment.
Dear, could I have done so, then my right hand…
Saplings freshly leaved
from smooth crotches prink their self-blessing groves.
Tut ankh aten, at eleven Tut ankh amun,
moved the capital back upriver to Thebes,
plowing under the revolution, but the army buried
the entire Amarna episode. His bride KV21A
among the forensic candidates,
her index finger skyward over the carotid,
waited until the gene team undid
her obscure tenancy up-valley and up-slope,
she who was married first to the saboteur,
then to the co-regent, then to brother Tut,
then briefly it seems to her maternal granddad,
all starting at age eight,
heavy-laden our nature when crowned, to survive
life on the heights: that *nature* which Edison,
dismantling the connections and rewiring them, insinuated
had *never been seen as one woman.*

23

The Polish Woods behind the Polish-American
technical college on the hill back of our house:
wispy hemlock sprays, a stone grotto
over a dribbling pipe at the spring, trails
in-winding, cleavage meanders of water
through sliding shade: these remain quick
behind the discovery
that the Hotel Ryder, burnt in the '30s up there,
hosted the world chess tourney in '04.
Emmanuel Lasker nearly missed winning that time.
His Queen Sacrifice was as deliberate
as his trek to another U.S. meet,
rappelling ant-size down
the side of a Finnish freighter onto ice
thence walking to Denmark and entraining
to Hamburg for the steamer. Handing over
the Queen remains one very nice piece of work,
obeisance to obtain conquest,
with Hilbert prodding him to the degree in math,
and Einstein chatting up that sly gaze,
sister-in-law Elsa playing busker to Gottfried Benn
then stitching her head back on and walking.
His tousled forelock and mustache
with the emigrés through those hemlocks hive love there.

24

Bilgamesh had already, with sidekick,
eliminated that brute on Cedar Mountain
and pillaged the trunks, when finally out on the end
of his string, past the map's border
on fogged ice cracking,
it was just possible for him to make out
the crash that a giant perpetrates when no one
is there to hear the thing fall.
String's end is rope's last twist from hawser's
fraying, and if you roll that filament
in your fingers, cadenzas all yours will come.
No private voicing meant to be overheard
ever was heard until first being vetted
by mind behind velvet. Yours, herma-Hermes.
Sappho's mortuary sound studio
and cricket-cage mausoleum, scratches
as mentis mentem tiny then huge, besotted
while stratosphere-clear—as real and as hard
as this place stitching wonders through the terrible.
And as empty, and as full,
and as unconquerable, and as defeated.
With eyes partly open, angled slightly below,
or closed and waiting on expanding terms,
I hear what I said thinning up the dawn beaches.

25

Contraction—a scoping down toward essence—
accelerates while the wiring vanishes:
fate, though staying, is not saying
just where, and the searchers
bend low, side-to-side brooding
left, right, swinging around to re-browse,
the gaze a metal detector with no boot.
Shall your heart be also! The scouts of fabled
miniaturization were idolators
of the massive: railroaders in twelve-volt
tugs of archaic tonnage—coal, steel, cement,
timber through fake tunnels across trusses between
peaks of plaster-on-wire. Pipe-cleaner trunks,
Doug Fir, Loblolly Pine—John Allen conjured these
as the bindu, smaller than small, greater than great.
Taking his guests downstairs for operations
on the *Gorre and Daphetid*, he never answered their questions.
Days after his death those unleaving groves
went up in a house fire.
Already pointing down into
the condensed realm, showing the way in the era
of the swollen and spreading, with Shiva's light smears of ash
and bone-yard vacancy they went on through, leaving
the questionable for the inconceivable.

26

That which from the mineral into swayings
piles up through orbital fire, bores into basis,
veins itself with drink, sheathes with callus,
here shades the ant. That which diameters
darkness turpentining manifest push.
Which from Gothic morphs through tensegrity
to floating feelers sucking in carbon and oozing
isotopes of Greek Fire, trading lung waste
for jet fuel. That which coffers the trousseau
of Maria de' Medici and Lincoln's bones.
The seven lamps of architecture kindle
and extinguish along its resinous
radius. That which declares itself single
and integral, defending the eld, paneling
boardrooms and catafalques,
tendrils here through anchorage.
Spindles territory into maps. Seethes with camphor.
Ties off the below with azure in a frondy tourniquet
loosened only by storm or chainsaw.
Cantilevering moons, it breathes out. Spining
suns with pond-rippled calendars, it breathes in.
Has no image of itself save its seed.
Will light out for Norway in the Big Heat
while stemming farther into the mountain. Will. And thus is.

27

Determination may contrive occasion but cannot
script the denouement. Emerson in age
bolted from his desk seized by the influx
one more time at maximum, the same as in youth
fuse-popping making him grin
in the only prayer of thanks a roof rod knows.
Pacing the upstairs puncheons, who cares the outcome.
Saw a stone tower once sheathing lightning
for what seemed minutes, the windows blown out
but mortar holding its shaking length, and knew
this branded me, but sensed the presumption of reading
that juice in cross-section. Concussion on no one's clock.
Benvenuto Cellini's father stood bowing his viol
and singing in their cellar
near the laundry's waning log fire.
Five, the son remembered the cold
and how his father called him and his sister
below stairs as soon as he had seen the thing,
a salamander cavorting
in the core-blue coals. And struck the future
goldsmith on the ears, soothing him
and giving him coins, explaining: he must always
remember this monstrance, unreported
by any man known to him in their own time.

28

Send him past your limit, the urchin courage
in the Kurd kid hired by Rawlinson
soon of the Afghan Wars, who once rode
750 miles in two weeks solo,
to venture past the gap in the ledge at Behistun
beneath which a rock wall towered
chiseled with the Akkadian list of kings
in trilingual array, shadows punching
chicken feet up and sideways along the scarp,
where a gap-spanning ladder
sprung loose and Rawlinson had to inch back. Skittering
bug-like over the surface, the boy got
a paper pressing of the passage.
Rawlinson's aide George Smith 40 years later, 1875,
psyched out the Cedar Mountain episode
as central to an epic about Nimrod—Izdubar—
tablet 5, the Flood—thus Jung's Izdubar, Gilgamesh
in the day of the stuttering mitrailleuse and the first
trough-lip churning tanks.
Between murder's hopped-up pace and ant-crawl philology,
between Pound's cameo
in Montale's hand after the Florence flood
and the seed archive in Norway's deep freeze,
zaps the electrode. Courage counts, mine—but read it?

29

Cartons of manila folders filled by
graph paper streaming with Father's cursive
print edge to edge
filled the rear half of a double garage
windowless, shaded on the north by alders.
The summer before college
he set them on sawhorses under bare lights
and paid me to sort and even segregate
for his quick hand to the fire.
Pages to or about Tesla, Vannevar Bush,
Von Neumann, Rickover—I hope not those
crinkling as the band of gray climbed each page
under a leaping orange line.
Though there they were in the deck. Jack of Hearts, Queen:
pencil-blue Pythagorean grids, steeper
through those weeks, did not hover
over Heidegger or bless Mondrian or elate
Simone Weil, but numbingly disclosed
other heights. The Mountain. Cedars spindling
mist-drift through some infant ice age. And his keen
Leonardo-ing, his cross-process
cross-industry management, were deployed too early
to come into play in some breakout from metaled
malice and tornado famines. If we break out.

30

Young Lovelock, saved by Uncle Leakey's moves,
swerved his accent from Brixton Trade:
It's not the hunting that hurts the horses' hoofs
but the hammer hammer hammer of the hard high road!
Taught myself to read
from headlines when nights piled one on the other
capitals in parade huge, orange,
thunder-smothered. Svenbro brought his pastor
father his first scribbles, and the shine there, the lather
of meaning, pulled him. You draw the light
from our effort, but the charge, your charge goes hard:
whom I dare apostrophize with the phonemes
that shook the hill-line of sleep and luridly
mocked scale as you slanted them forward
like Zouaves under field packs.
You who elude and invade and escape and empty
nomination, Eckhart's glide-zero
in the only testimony that calms me
while detonating, soundlessly each time—
your charge breaks the languages
as the short unshaven man did waving his arms
when we plumbed the Gotthard—
a Swiss once assigned to German trains
through that same tunnel, to sniff out the verboten:
I all us upblow, even I only ein guard.

31

The right actor in a wrong mise en scène,
like Schopenhauer's analysis of walking,
is breaking his fall all the time.
But here, daring to slow—
urgency stays marrow-central with that,
bearing down on those
who remain timely only in their bristling
incapacity to move faster
into the minute, so gristly
is their occupancy of it, the folk
without clocks. Vigilers of the upwelling.
Who span not only Cuzco's
seamed ramparts and slumping stone walls
through woodlots uproad, but also
the cedar blip near Beirut
with Europe and Africa at night from the cold lob
of six miles:
spokes from London, Berlin, Cairo, and Rome's
fascinations, not the undead
but all who in this wink
burn, or turn to each other,
or perceive, or think: freshest
though old as elves,
foretime of the eye before it judges—

32

then swing, the eastern corridor
past inky Atlantic;
out from Chicago, spidery; Vegas, luminous
surf creaming the West Coast—
across the full range of the familiar,
the dangerous,
toylike, and strange.
Not feeling it before, this shudder
in ontic headwinds, but waking to joins
brighter between the blocks yet their ice
still black, not yet blue powder—
my house mortared sparklingly, all my scenes
thrust far off while plenum spills through.
Bubbles crowding toward break-shine, squirming to get there,
jostle until free agents clear the pack
streaking, heralds from below.
And through murk, that has been the prodigious
disclosure: falling as being pulled,
dragged as breaking surface and gulping flame.
That is the forest: the eld pushing green
yet tough as a bitch taking hounds. One through all contraries:
abruptly unwadding newsprint around a heart
under a streetlamp, that close though separate,
always it has no contemporaries.

33

Rolling shadows inshore,
silvery above them, sandy beneath, the real
unrolls the stream beds it also swims.
In a brook past the window, after the doctor
stepped out, a blue origami thing abruptly
stood waiting—as double Orpheus had for his spiritus rector
duplex Hermes while wading the drag road
up from basement cognition—his loss turning more
on the human gap in my courage, lamentable
though real, than on some weakly soldered
nerve in that bird. The doctor returning stuttered
as I motioned silence—*What's th - that!*—and I said, *That*
is a blue heron.
As Oscar Milosz, 1916,
was visited by a sun from below, condenser
of spaces into its hyper-point, before their release
into blood—movement prior to anything
that moves, loving prior to what loves—
blood hull of number, of Yes and No, rocking already
in its own sea. Is it idleness
to mull his cadences while so much else
occupies the scene—rightly, the loud skēnē—
bright shadows, squirrels jerking upright to nibble
while I must, in our forest, dine on myself.

34

Gambits, when the game's hidden? My god,
my God is what hearing seeing and tasting
spurt from so as to open to its resurgence,
wet face at the smalls not only the majors, rivered
cheek in sun noiseless leaf-sharp firing up.
Heads I win, tails I win again.
Winning, that misfire. But catching you in play
with both faces at once, then I get somewhere,
the red-green off-on of an airliner
at night, that slinky sequining
through boudoir softness, slideaway.
Not that one hoards technique
in this era like Jean Bodin's.
Then, wars of religion stoked the horizon,
now, less focused, we make more smoke, yet he's right:
the best of universal law lies hidden.
So, blatant, babble his Parisian shoe
whispering over cobbles as the one thing
that ought to tease my ears: suede, globo-historical,
monarchist only to stop the killing. Real.
What is not hidden, the squeeze, obliging duties
machine-tooled to meet and press in on each other,
also leave us plain to each other. Evident.
Slowly, out here, pressing toward something solid.

35

Came in the panopticon, Bentham's titration,
and the vacuum tube through Raytheon
on into governance. Vannevar Bush's rectifier
enlarging to the firm's wide gaze, he of the Project,
then Memex and on to hyperlinks
as if in penance, his company Lux Dei penetrating tanks
and bunkers and the questionable homes
of mannunkind. At last troubled, he radioed your station—
you, we say, as acolytes minding electrons
in magnum mysterium—radioed your haze,
your messaging blitz. We awaits.
And this is no recital for the sake
of itemizing those close-at-hand factors
of both complicity and fascination,
familial, patrilineal, and common
as the shared-out breath, in order prick-a-prick
to secure booster shots for my immune system.
But rather to say that these, Jack, are the trees
that inhibit my view of the woods. At Shaker Hancock,
saw their tools and sales moxie, not the regimental
abandon of their dancing. That spidery hickory hay fork
cupping upward in rooms for the hired men—
unlaced bussel easing light forth—Lebanon,
your mound, tall in heat ripple, we do know you.

36

Samhain, banquet of the Two Ways,
out of deeper colors, into deeper cold,
your franchise cleaver-shiny
across the Max Beerbohm wish for dignity
in a butternut squash, that whack requiring
mallet-taps to open onto the slickery
gold hoard of reassurances from the morticians
after they've readied skinny Akhenaten, plum rump
trailing a sagging belly, for the fate of a strung pullet.
Half-eaten beetroot centering the carnage, every plate holy,
one of the thin places, alright! Thus for us thick folk
a Breughelesque occasion.
Pound's carved profile still with Montale after
the Arno crested in '67
remains my bookmark in spite of the hell-shine on it—
smeared and stained for good, yet also for probative good
a gondola freighted with residents rounding one corner
poling, peering, for no one has yet found
the trashy yellow paperback with diagrams
of infant Osiris and his great twin sister copulating
in the womb: Egypt in Italy, Italy in lower Manhattan,
seeding their royal broth in the muck of some river bank.
Not simply October 1923 Year Two of the New Order
in the here-and-now. That's Vico's old wind-up clock.

37

Sokurov has filmed farewell to Europa at the Winter Palace
in the Hermitage, his tall fool from the eighteenth century,
a diplomat in black, no lace, catching aromas from the Dutch Masters,
and at the ball whirling in mazurkas with plumed partners
after which applause for the orchestra and exit down both wings
of the great stairs, bemedaled sashes, the gartered stream
of the dead in living flood, sideburned Pushkin there, dixit.
Pushpin! the jab going in with feeling, for anything that was an object
has become a relation drawn out and lingering, for sale
yet ungraspable. John Marriner at Ani was on its track too, sealing
candle gleam over chant at young Gagik's coronation
beneath the dome's hole, rain misting rubble. Yet it won't do,
staging these reviews—don't ask us what we are screening,
ask us how, if we are lucky, we look past. For then the knife hangs,
no one moves, and yet Gretchen must not die. Dismantling this,
untying the fly, unlacing Smoking Joe Frazier's eight-ounce gloves,
are stipulated for philosophers from here on out. Tapping for air
in the fished-out nose cone: punch through to her!
White embroidery on the furze,
the same on the inch's window, and I have that hostage
to warm and salve for an hour. *Late,* weirds the crow,
Great. Spate. I shall be loud among the loud
but slur among her sands, and crowd
to the plunge between them, and cleanse, and begin to gnaw.

38

Peter Birkhäuser's painting was reset
only by maximum stretch—the crackled skull
of Pierre Curie suddenly his own, muttering
directions to finding that yellow pulp novel
with the diagrams: something that grotesque,
you flame it, you blame it, but one sure thing is
that at first you won't grock him. In fact, she says so,
in his dream a stone woman crying out for release—
her pubis had defeated the carver, who notched it with
the scales of Libra, in months of Great Year
the dawn of farming and cities, whole-body sensing
in the hunter by then fading.
At this juncture, though politeness will still prevail,
within the hour everyone with position
will politely vacate. Studious colleagues
and those with a tested voice in the choir: all cleared out,
back to tracking parades of civics
toward the couches and porte-cochères
of mononucleosis. Yet abyssal
intelligence inheres not only in *Starry Vere*
but starry labia, source petals out past instinct
and fumbling hands. Radiation
streaming the lifespans, breeder reactor, pubic
root to leaf from galactic dark.

39

Whoever submits to future unknowns controls
present inconceivables. Orwell knew better
than to put it that way—yet grasping him means
releasing handholds on open balance.
Walking on ice with a blowtorch
fearless of immersion. When the temples of Isis
were shuttered by codifiers
of transcendence, they barred entry to Goethe
and to more of my own kit than I knew—his gift
for public administration nowhere in mine,
but to him no solace for the sadness and illness
that followed from going into grand harness
and treading out civic oats. For who knows
what that cult encoded
of human futures—each cedar pillar both
the meme of lightning and resistance to it—
gale force confronted, minutes of it volting
down the tower, or down-up, rivering both ways,
windows blown, blocks in spasm still glued,
stacked levels and outlooks—the goal, aereated solid—
jellied in seizure jimmying any axis,
too-much enough. But then the everywhere
gossamer of wave brought your inrush. Cunny
of all darks, fire rising in The Dog.

40

The busheled ingathering of all lives,
apo kata stasis, restoration
of all the poured-out blood and sap variations:
theology's scoped dream of biology's crepitant
and thrashing slog through aeons
squeezes one long painful birth—and that means origin
in all of its ends, awake.
Summary percolating the sludge of slow tryout,
such may be—but if so, then the sludge debt
must be paid to the last penny.
All this whispers root to the topmost leaf, pulled
cell-wide up the mash capillaries, out
each leaf-thick channel end: green to you,
blue or black to the ant, but in esse
cognitio matutina, sun as the moon face
of rising. Seed to cedar ramifying
up through racks of cloud ruckled by light
frames morning knowledge irresistibly crowning
from dark eld—against irreversibles
clouding that churn we drank from, a daimon
cranking the lithe line out of Chauvet,
haunch and mane one wire,
thus Plato's horde gulp from that river, shales bouncing,
lightning striking birth sparks upward through smoke.

41

Subtle and more subtle grow the temptations.
I heard this evening evening's aubade, the crush
of radiance in on itself,
crumpling worlds with the pyreia Archimedes
threw at the Fifth Fleet, marsh sea pinks at dawn.
And heard gongs tapering to hush among slaughters
pre-tallied by the Hoseas. Real meeting
crowds now into these bi-valences—medicine
vaporizing, bleeps flurrying the dead zone—
to notch the choice tighter: adoration
or Selbstmord. Short of that, torpor after wrath,
then rage after torpor, both humiliating—
mucked manhood near,
too near, all the controls. The plighting
between woman and this has not yet chalked
its limit. Teens in the caves painting,
their genius of outering—those firsters
did early Balanchine slanting
past my grasp, no artifact but freed movement
balancing the berserking act between
heart and wall. Bog sunset, berry-float sheen,
dollop of early moon in her, I break
as the blurred bear wading in to trawl.

42

I heard this morning, waking into the level
red radiance decanting me, the gravel
rolled by basement rivers, basses and baritones
overlapping, steady as a sans culotte
knitting during windless climbs of the thing
into its slit, herms from harms: male force
yarning out the female demand: *Wait!*
ductile stretch winnowing the contract: *No terms!*
neither the underwater monks of dispersed Tibet
nor the choirs of Novgorod, but the singlet
on a runner rippling for the tape at full push
as his core plays his nerve like a string bass,
plucking while sleeving the input ratio
from thrusted mass while flowing with seed's torque—
not my hang-back when I first went out on the wire
toward a soft hand, not quite hearing,
only later past fatigue, its breathing:
I thought you would never come! Thus that rag
across my cock swathing piston thighs
opening to blood
at ram speed while every bone bowed:
waking past the Lost Colony, bearing down
without mitigation on the axle's held roar
and therefore not haunting the phantom groves—

43

—not standing with the two London schoolteachers
who found themselves with Marie Antoinette
and her court dressed as villagers close by
the faux drip-drip watermill, and saw children
trundling hoops in the same sunlight
that held them all there before the First War,
Verdun and Wipers. Neither haunting
the ghost trunks at origin nor fingering their shag armor,
not craning my neck back
to scan diameter arrays of lit green
in fans interpenetrating. Nor compounding
their gone sap with mystic blood, Milosz's
revelation, primal unity bulbing
from the ruby on the pectoral. Nor blood coaxed fuller,
Faust-mitted engineers
crafting it to throng more redly, thickly,
erythropoietin ginning the mix, poiein
curdling the hearts in racers who keel over
their handlebars: Goethe missed that wrinkle,
poiesis of the groves turned into speed sludge
for overtaking origin to replant it,
tail in mouth, yet that circle birthing
the unrooted, a rhizome
a-swish in the grab elegy of conquest.

44

Watching spurts through gaps in the tall sheds
at Jones & Laughlin on Monongahela
at night, efflux rippling those slits, ingots
trundling beneath whams of the sledge, shedding
sparks smeared down water—too early to forget,
too late to keep, gone technē—made distant clangs
my tuning fork for germlines of the unforged:
vulnerable seed like the palm scattering it
must spray untampered if it too is to valley
its line of life. It, and the blundering ages:
nothing less chancy will dress shoulders with altar cloths
still iced by winds off the Cuillins and still warm
from offering the unwithheld.
An acorn pried from its dirt jacket lashes a bullwhip
to one side seeking purchase, to the other
it fans baby leaves, the khaki vest
unhinging across meaty red, a testicle
putting itself to the knife because it was everything
but now bursts in fallout, the three ages
or seven ages of man kaput, rife in scarlet,
cut down at the throne. No one knows how the bridge
slides underfoot. How the station, the track
are assigned, and that rocking glide, smeary glass
over steaming roofs passing, day fresh. Not one.

45

Devising herding tactics for swordfish, Hemingway
backed the *Pilar* toward them in mid-chase,
the Chrysler Crown's rumble through planked white cedar
at 70 horsepower, throated for
the tugging kill now eating its own exhaust
in a supreme counter-move.
But when he dug in at Ketchum after scuttling
towering bookcases in his Cuban study,
they backed onto *him*. His Boswell
would not credit it at the time. But clearing accounts
much later he confirmed that the Bureau hounded
that morose man, tapping the phones in his room
during treatment—*Scarce can endure delay*
of execution. Trochees hobble the dactylic
forward thrust of the line, pitching downward
damned below Judas; more abhorred than he was.
And so, with the largo of civics, you may chew on
its nut in the stipulated cocktail, two limes
and the juice of half a grapefruit demitted
into the iced mash of a *Papa doble*,
to afford misery shelter
past Cowper's masteries, beyond Idaho's,
over the mountains on a clear day and away,
drinking it back thus, keenly draining backwash—

46

—for the hunt is pursued without sentiment
though with Waugh's theologic on ruling passions.
In Shakespeare's old age the Virginia Company
dispatched vignerons from Languedoc
to assess the cash reach of those vines tendrilling
the wilderness. Further, not only arbors
of silver and gold screened by scree glinting
the front range—that could be gouged out—but what
the Boss sensed in old Gutiérrez
weeping and turning away when the super-marlin
spun full off the stern fleeing. The animal
powering into solitude singularly
accompanies the man in vigor and persistence,
and the openings outpace seeing or saying: the Andromeda
Galaxy cartwheels through
one night's white cedars
as that procession of whales tempo rubato
into Melville, parallax tricks reserved for
each Bilgamesh going at it
as if starting with his own springboard. The route to the roots
drinks meaning—*What use is the sailfish's sail to that fish?*
Why do marlin always travel east to west
against the current? Fowler named one species
of sculpin for the Boss. Wings, those bait-loaded outriggers.

47

Pharaoh-like pose, knees bare and hands floating
aligned along your thighs, shining once more
but here for the last time—poof!—ignites no burner
nor pronounces the spell over,
but rewinds, reminds: even clasped,
knees of the gods array powers
against which I stand no chance if I run from
my devil. So the clash only seems
unresolved: every laurel atomized
and blown by agnostic earnestness—agnosia
before, agnosia behind, agnosia
all around—blesses fuse and rammed plunger,
snowing the oncoming. Known, your name still leaves
your nature snubbed, offended,
knowledge still puny before power. Which shoulders
the crocus in March, October's red vines—
tenth month, hard on the ninth wave—while holding a mirror
to my face as it walks me off the cliff.
You climbed in the flame but were not its hoarded resins—
none of your sisters rode the whoosh gusher
pluming fields downwind with black happiness.
The clavichord's knees, hinged like a heron's
transmit the action from where they are, not who.
Who: miniscule, indispensable variable.

48

Spooks, profiteers, and bouncers not only hold hands
but sleep and wake together—the Western
Shangri-La, mythology no longer dreamed
but acted coldly—compelling me not only
to fight them off but freight my shelves with them,
making my house theirs, a snail's slobbering weight.
If soul were the ooze from that, bottling it
would gain me unstoppered life. Yet only with all lights
extinguished does the cor altum win
elbows sharp for Liban,
wordless voice in day-long breathing—no stairs
took Minas up from Arno lugging his lopped head,
no shrine waited, but a snail paving sandpaper.
How gradual, man's light—the heart snatched by some power—
yet through a late door in leaf-thick May
spreads return, the house attentive, and facing it there
the high heart, a rumpled crest—the serene
spine of Himalayan Appalachia,
Juniata, all known, all welcome. Ganging
exigency that leans everywhere
into everything comes from behind in strobic
flashes of spring, early autumn, spring, early autumn,
stutters of greeny-orange tilting me, and through
the crack thus worked open pours out what is.

49

Forget angels, the powers love our suffering.
Penance, penthos, not capes blown over
figures in the images—valor, fidelity, fight—
but rippled orange in a Nor'easter, nylon
lashing staccato against my ears in the glisten.
A poncho not a promotion, sack flapping suit
to laggard honor. The stagger
of advance, chill hissing and damp totter as sky
uncrumples even while it drenches, tissue
around a gift whitely mountainous
crackling the vast upward while I lean here.
Above and below are back in the hole baking,
swelling their enzyme grenades. Temples emerging
at Göbekli Tepe, acres of fox and boar,
crane and scorpion on hammerhead pillars,
were buried by their builders as soon as finished.
And no houses: constant repetition
and simplification, but no dwelling. So now
that I've learned to drop past the crib where I stood
gripping while sleepless, through the floor of a grown man's house
and land past Dresden, Kolyma, preverbal water
somewhere nearby, I thank you fervently
but do not reach out. For you too, mortal though trunked
around bristlecone and Kew Gardens tungsten,
must stand it, memorious through the night watch.

50

For docks, decks, hull planking, fences: white cedar,
Arbor vitae, trailer stock from the booty
to Uruk, erected in gateposts and doors, first frame
for passage, interdiction. Valve of our story.
Some of you is here, some in legend, psalm—
matter then anti-matter. Paul Dirac
completed the world by imagining the pinprick realm
as a Tesla Coil wigging out,
his acute algebra coming later. Seeing it
is elder theory—going to the games
or at night down to the Piraeus to watch
a torch race on horseback for savage Bendis, anti-matter
from Thrace. Dirac was quiet about it all
when his buckshot squirreled the cosmic ray photos.
Sokrates didn't mention the torch business
once waylaid by his Andrew-Carnegie host
and held as *prisoner-of-war* on the way back up.
What have they done to my beautiful physics! bawled Pauli
fleeing back to Schweiz from Trinity-land.
The very grain of your sawn fiber reeks
with resinous counter-sensing. So, tree is stone—
one way of seeing roots through another, such that
if stones sweat blood and trunks bead turps in sirocco,
between them the gap, manifesting, crackles.

51

The canyon's lip on the kiss of space—the level
would have to tilt backward so that one might
walk down the scarp: such is the perspectival
zaniness that comes from being able
to launch across the room with elephant tusks
at bankers and pols presto but then, standing,
find both eyes finely, painlessly slashed.
The rhino's in me but I'm not quite in him.
May slosh into the direct current, but turn
back to the account books through cold
Rubicon I may not: something keen past drenching
attaches, propels, dripping from stirrup and pizzle.
It's not the gleaming torrent but the thread in it
as if the gap's tracery, that decides.
That blesses both territories either side
while punching my transfer ticket, click-click.
An oven slice of pocky sourdough moon
still sun-warm wakes the hand to Paleolithic
tassles in wind-toss and seed-bag. Pandora's fling
into the furrow, its ridge wall a granary
then a stockade against siege: wars born there.
And where irreversibles clot them into the plasm
of winning, the man in the back seat en route
to the ceremony whispers *Mortis!*

52

The stairs late in my vision were no tree.
A boy of five had become my charge—motionless sea stilling me,
the rim half-lit for hours, morning knowledge withheld,
sky, sea, and littoral
a blush rising, the mauve of blown rose.
Nameless and thick, eros veiled in the cosmos.
Then his hand in mine. And panthers padding
around us, the same color, closing in,
companioning us, shoulders pistoning
softly in their pelts, they too looking out
to the line across that glow. How fear rose up
nothing reminds: it was mostly for him,
then finding the stairway behind us, and climbing
back into this zone where threat is assured.
Whereas
misperception did not snare Noël Pierre:
a foggy pit, lagoons sheeting the basis,
a vast trunk at the node of things, catalpa hung
with hearts of the dead. No civic strong men
hoisting the human pyramid onto their shoulders,
nor sheet-gold Agamemnon's crumpled eyes.
But winking sages in the limbs' crotches,
citadel of the worlds. He had joined a crowd
swirled down a funnel. And was not afraid.

53

Hearne in *Journey to the Northern Ocean* nailed it:
fire rips open seeds dormant in loam
beneath pine duff, and Thoreau watered them with observation,
who nearly burned out Concord
with a campfire by the river: two miles of woods,
and he running ahead to warn them. Henry an alias, Henricus, Hawrex,
Haganrih, king of the close—in that respect a brawl-mate
of the melt-phase bankers torching our commons.
Writers do not mention now Pound their scourge (*Anti-Semite*)—
a blackened floor, the paisa' in Bogliasco
their spokesman: *Ez didna know WHAT he was DOIN'*—
no chirp, crick, hiss.   *Then the trees appealed to the thorn bush:*
Rule us! And the thorn answered, If you anoint me truly,
then shelter in my shade—but deceive me and fire will spurt from these thorns
and eat up the cedars of Liban.
His King Wings the Monarchs, paisley silk cravats
wintering on Mexican fir trunks clear-cut or doomed to crisp
in thirty years, half-ounce weather vanes for world tilt—
Abimelech on Hudson, Abimelech
on Potomac, it is too easy to pronounce
roll call on the clones: let them show each other
lightness in a handful of ash. Rather track Jotham
lighting out with seed manuals and a bag of bread and raisins
for whale-gray Wachusett.

54

Or was it misperception?—
the heart first sees eros veiled in the cosmos
and then what Boehme saw:
ardet non lucet,
it burns but gives no light, acetylene
siphoning up the wick of wrath whole
to spill wholesale in due time, God's uthuh chillun
emptying the playground
as with the wigged-out night watchman on Patmos:
thus my pards on coiled haunches,
their brownish pink pelts
kindling far down in
vires acres Luciferi Aquarius accendit—
dire powers of the light-bearer
torched by the water-bearer—
thus into their shoulders from under
that wide water ledge
goes that glow also,
waterfire ignition just offstage,
the footlights there beginning to come up
to love waiting, to fear waiting,
to the option, to the necessity,
thus rolls that gleam into the mute
rocking of their shoulders.

55

The man who strode into the heat
of misprision and delusion
to protest, to no avail, that he was not
the spy who came in from the cold—
for MI6 had, after all, approved publication—
walks head-down plastered by the wet leaves
of tribal fantasy. Of ripe refusals to shake
fixations on the endless tomography of Red.
To the wizards whom he despised, the Hitler war
had been a distraction. Induct General Gehlen into CIA,
billet him in Bormann's old villa—
thus no mystery inheres in the plot, it must hang out
in the elusively linking thing—
thus Katharine Washburn to me: *Send me your versions*
of Andreas Gryphius, yours and John le Carré's are the only ones.
En route to Manhattan le Carré's sole typescript
went missing, no incriminating copy
lingering at headquarters in Cornwall.
Thus mid-Atlantic or midair, his contact still leans
into the prevailing Westerlies
undebriefed in a wind-smeared cloak,
jet-stream ligamentum corporis et animae
from Luther's *world full of devils* but without Luther's *as if,*
mindful of streets turned to *conduits of blood.*

56

The good, antagonist of the better, goads betterment
from itself as someone other:
trunk upward against bole in a race for light.
The predator escalator
in that way ignores prey—force turns to seeking,
Marcus preferring his teacher
to any other thing, or other one, rocking together with him
in the violent ambuscade of eternity,
piled foliage and spindrift. Sink in that ruck
and I jive to Schrödinger with his Hölderlin and adultery
holed up in Clontarf, space-time the Irish Sea.
Even that acolyte of the *Principia*
got right spirit subtly amiss, even they
of his guild not wanting to hear Pauli, and Pauli
not wishing really to tell them, *The soul is in this our fascination*
as if in a 6-D cement mixer,
I choke to disclose it. Epictetus, former slave,
tutored Marcus about his crystal set,
its crackling transmissions, but Marcus got it better
about the two natures, convening across parsecs
at the supervening, meant-to-be
crossroads that we are. A Chinese woman ushered
Pauli in his dreams
to the lectern where he gripped the rails and then balked.

57

Shipwrecks grabbed at Hopkins, Mallarmé, Ungaretti,
architecture at Ruskin, Pound, Davie,
slaveries of every degree and order, and order, Melville—
and all, like other diggers during the long
crepuscule of the revolutions,
wrestled through umbrageous skirts of Isis
into slivers of daylight, the muck forests
of thrown-off jealous mother,
materia prima, muck enclosure, materia cardia—
root-sleeving clay for the supervenient
breakout, slither-shoots through humus, green
as mineral wet promises green even
prior to emergence. *They will chew on rocks*
prophesied teenager Rimbaud,
souring that gleam.
Dirac gnawed theoretically on cosmic number ratios
that foresaw confirmation of origin point's
blow-out cataclysm: no labs, nothing
but focus. Dining next to him at St. John's,
the archaeologist knew that he could not simply
pop a question about the physicist's
views on Stonehenge. *Have you been to the theater*
or the cinema this week? Dirac's smile was meant
to be friendly. *Why do you wish to know?*

58

When two barges of Pinkertons
docked at the Homestead Works to seal Frick's lockout
(It's yours now, President Harrison, out of my hands)
it is stop-action in my inner theater:
a young Dutch-American down-river
steps from a glass-blower's shed. The Saturday shift is ending
and he lights his weekly cigar.
In eleven years he will pilot freights on the Pennsy mainline
past Altoona through the Horseshoe Curve.
Each train is a ship. He will be its captain
and a union man. Because he is also a scamp
I set him among those other lively dead
who torch oil drums on a flatcar and release the brakes downhill
toward those barges,
that load crumpling the thing when it hits the flats
burning out uselessly. But shifting the terms: such is magic!
Would he have put his hand to that? And, paterfamilias
ten years later, would he have grinned with relief?
Such is the hermetic stress test
that George Bellows, my painter, would have me administer to
my progenitor: bypass solar oracles and stiff the management
as the brat with the tortoise-shell guitar.
The dead's very boom-box: *Here, Apollo, you play it.*

59

Pure Havana hand-rolled, each Saturday—
his first probably at eighteen, with two thousand gone
dynamiting tunnels, driving piles, blasting cuts
by the time Vanderbilt sold out to Morgan
and sank Carnegie's South Pennsylvania Line,
a cougar shadowing pools
in the dripping bore, Kittatinny.
Plits magnified in the stone mouth.
The trick was not Morgan's via Vanderbilt
but the first move in poésie moderne,
cargo transfers, bills of lading rewritten.
A puddler pokes iron slivers down into slag
like frost spars glowing white hot—
more valuable than the furnaces, the fires
which must not go out.
Fresh barbed wire lashed the drowned from Johnstown,
a parasol of it on Frick's three-mile fort at the Works,
shiny coils of it on Herman's freights
porting its litters to new pastures.
His old man's knees pleated gray meet my small hands
as he lights up once more, encore performance,
framing O then blowing them past my reach,
rings: furled curtains self-lifting around a void action,
revolving inward traveling, traveling by unfolding.

60

Through old pasture road to a siding for tilt hoppers,
at four peering from pillows in the front seat,
with Father the furnace wizard pointing as slag ruptures
to orange, cinnabar, shiny black.
Such are the antipodes of my pastorals:
untended meadows soon to be parceled,
and disheveled powers seeking repose, as if
setting building stones next to the dead sans inscriptions.
Gleams of foundation
cascade through clinker into grass,
slumping to vein darker, the revealed
jelling in hiddenness. For one moment
there is nothing that has not opened.
What I say to you in darkness
speak in the light, field slag the builders rejected.
Kid Archilochus at the smooth stones
in a meadow where his father sent him
to sell a cow, meets smooth-spoken women
who say they will buy it
then disappear, the heifer with them.
At his feet, a lyre.
Inlay still shiny-black these 68 years.

61

To stand in the throttle bay of a Consolidation
is to face the firebox at eighteen inches,
wind and rain from the steel window ledge,
with boiler and firebox plumes
piling away overhead.
Sayenga pulled pranks on his brakeman and fireman. And so
when the fireman got down once at the crossing
which they blocked every Wednesday for ten minutes
when making up the train in a branch yard,
he waved his arms and ran. *Help! He's beating me!*
Car doors open, a crowd forms.
Herm notches out the throttle, flourishing his kerchief
and laughing: *Minetti, you jackass, get back in here.*
Whereas Frick simply left. And wiped out unions for forty years.
There is no labor that does not play out its mastery
in peril, a glistening Hungarian
rabbling the open hearths, leaping.
Panther, apex predator on phantasmal
suede pads, you are both him and the boss.
Or Shklovsky's Tolstoy, field marshal of solitude
reshaping the world just there
in Kittatinny's undressed bore, that forlorn penetration:
guzzling slope-necked and matte gold
from puddled runoff.

62

The immense undigested default,
half-veiled, half-blatant ignorance
shrugged off like water, thick shame before posterity,
the roweled book of the Kinds,
and the eye at morning.
John Dee, I recall from his dream records,
astrologer-adviser to young Elizabeth,
found himself more than once at the North Pole
doing intricate maths, discomfited by women,
his campsite littering wolf scat through geometry—
the equal of Cardano, leveraging Copernicus,
equipping Cabot with seamarks
and Britain precociously with the empire virus.
But able to let lodestar
galvanize the oldest and keenest in us?
Obsessed in the end with the sea, Winslow Homer cautioned
Paint only three waves
so there it sets us, where now blue ripple
mirrors 2 a.m. sun,
fresh mind-map for waylessness. All is a preparation.
John Prospero Dee abjured his whole kit:
obsidian Aztec mirror as spirit-catcher
and a unified field theory of nakedness
down to the last blush—

63

whose auguries might be those greeny-violet
auroras through night's north,
Fauviste silk scarves lashing
our sky to his, coherent
so that scoutmaster may at last crack his wand,
wizard wounded en route
to the unimpeachable
spindle formations, Staffa Cliffs of number
awash erect in phenomena
and crash glory. E. O. Wilson narrowed
scope to mere islands, life
percolating inside their rings,
yet even so, anxious dreams kept coming
from his South-Sea breakthroughs:
it's nearly time to leave but he has collected no ants,
most of them new species,
so he needs native forest, and spots trees but finds
a windbreak with houses, fields—then he's driving,
speeding past more settlements, toward mountains
far to the north—
in every dream always to the north.
Perhaps forest remains in the mountains.
I fumble with a map and locate the access road,
but I cannot go. My time has run out.

64

Taping a trunk's girth is child's play,
cable-joisting into the canopy a fooler
when it comes to penetration, and drilling
into the core layers for corollaries
makes for dense allusions. Arbor vitae
withstands winds even
as it surge-pumps capillaries,
but it is the decades-on dénouement
that best initiates one
into woodmanship:
in the fore-minded that last chapter is feeling,
its pursuit finally head-on,
the meaning that had blown past in act
coming in at the seams. Though at sap speed:
recognizable yet alien,
as rain on Bellerophon—
the sun-hugging planet in Pegasus—
drips from clouds of incandescing iron
streamlining down, the needle rain from drained hemlock
and souls in Doré's Dante
spilling from their bleachers
to restart the self-basting cookoff
uncoiling superheated
up sheath xylem, its thread tunnels, your tree.

65

Greece says that it needs 40 fighter jets.
Yet suddenly no one needs Greece. Syntagma Square
fills with paradigmatic trash and revolt.
The grammar of consent is screwed, the syntagms
of bond as pledge are battened by maniples
onto the peoples in rotation, screws in suits
to the beat from the oar master as forty nations
contest their debt packages but pull *ny a papai!*
edge-on into wave-heave. And recitation
de jure halts nothing in crimine. Fiat luxe.
Now for readiness of heart toward the biblos
of seed, that long book of ships tossed helter-skelter
each page and letter meant
to be strewn by the hammering calends, snow, sun,
glacier, esker, pond melt, parch crack, fires.
But flowers, tough vulvas of process, accelerated
the whole pace: their soft drumming, and right through
goes the germ's missile, caliber X the same
in the Valley of the Kings and freeze-dried in the Arctic.
My rain tub blue and huge
tilts to its low lip, through its ice disk the axe
smashes ringing, for when the core yanks forth its lining
and the bolt sizzles down, the whole air stretches a string
to the bow's whap, *Selah.*

66

Helen Nearing took her violin to Europe,
Krishnamurti proposed to her on the boat back,
but she went for Scott the Professor, who went after our life-ways
with masonry hammer. Fired out of his chair,
he built their stone house beneath Stratton, lecturing
cross-country to workers, not cowering then,
in age raising stone rooms two states closer to sunrise.
What have we not heard and ignored?
The blue poops of the galleons bobbed at Lisbon
behind the useless breakwater, the auroras
of a shaken winter unroll their snap and flash.
Nearing hauls water in a steel pail.
The structure of aluminum rays out
into the bauxite and copper steals in East Timor,
the slaughter lists for Jakarta sear in the siroccos of Iraq
laced with dust uranium, children's cancer wards
stripped of meds *usable as weapons*,
nor would Nearing have stepped clear of this giddy winefat,
shirt and overhauls stained with his own red.
Scrolls of the Northern Lights ripple at the pail's brim,
now haematose, now key lime,
sloshing the pole of inaccessibility
lodged in plain sight. I would rather not
have seen any of it, but I cannot forget.

67

Free of everything that has clung to me
because I grasped at it, submitted to the span
of the dominum sine pondere, indeed
not ponderable, nor shall the wind take me.
In the sagged valley of this cup breed microbes of remedy.
Below the air's rubbing and spin, either side
of shiftings among strata, over magma.
Potencies teem without cease, their frames recompose,
their joins lock the seams of keen bevels.
The years of shearing from them approach the runway
though the tower says *Not cleared, not yet.*
A threshold underfoot like any other,
rounded stone surfacing from earth,
its grain that of a muffin's poppy seeds,
its heave postulating submerged progressions
and its cracks filled grandfatherly, easy with wreckage,
nearby tussocks its Himalayas, weeds its bending palms,
a compact with all that is solid,
a treaty with convulsion, evolution,
at noon beneath the demon's dragged heel
and at sunset a bulge of burgundy,
its nap abraded then smooth with motion, wanting nothing,
vacant and undeceived,
the other face of stronghold.

68

Nah ist, und schwer zu fassen der Gott.
Render that
by way of China's seed pictures, and one gets
Close unholy riches crackle over fires, conning futures.
A short-tailed bird does not fly by day when yellow hardpan
lays out his breakfast. As the convincing climber
leans into slopes, so must you haul on your rope, tugging salt cable
home through the ninth wave. Thus teaches the sun's cord, and the moon's,
and stars ticking over with their vanishing reveals
and sliding alignments. Shen is not easy.
The incorruptible Yao Shen waits with his bow.
They moved the capital once: that card is out of the pack.
The entire superstructure tenses its joins,
oracles ratchet and chitter among turnbuckles,
yet night wind travels no faster among May branches
nor draws out any thinner its long breath:
Lindisfarne met the Viking axe, new Lindisfarne stalls in sweat lodges,
yet mica sinking in rock speeds the antlers
sharpened against it, Yao Shen
timing the strops: not warfare is his pressure
but an earth heaven-side out—it will dance me
to the slimming gap, my banner will pass to his grip
and he will snatch my drum, I shall yank on the arrow
protruding through the back of my head as I plunge
forward, the country vanishing between us.

69

Thus if a horse kicks at the traces,
if it upends the groom,
that very wildness, like the fresh rumor of order
in young manhood,
Garibaldi's, Bismarck's, believe it—
from a patchwork of duchies and prince-bishops
pouring to *Everything within the state,*
nothing outside the state, nothing against the state—
will herald, soberly or giddily, its opposite,
as carts for rushes did the Assyrian horse god.
Kantorowicz in sagging Weimar hailed the savior Frederick II
as Antichrist, as if helplessly
clearing the treasuries and trash compactors of the aeon.
Endarkening accelerations only blur beckoning
beacons, always here, ever receding.
I entered the elevator—glass, and outside—too late to back out—
beneath a team of aerialists, their whiskery poles,
guy wires tensing, nylon rippling the scarf
on the axial pianist with his amplified keyboard
doing rat-a-tat minor seconds,
a mere tinkling inside our hardened bubble, its plunge
tilting the figures, shrinking them, and abruptly
I feel myself breathing.

70

Fidelio means Leonore once a husk splits
and push administers what gain must not touch.
Do two hundred years of voices, chucked behind granite,
even through medieval mortar,
turn durance and rot to sweetness? Question wedges
statement through wet risk, soiled, rooting.
The muscle-bound Aztecs had battalions
yet their emperor saw in Cortés the blue-feathered End of Days,
and tuning galaxies, the twangs of Nemesis
stirred Herakles from his dithers bolt upright
into a seated burning. Which delusionary is ours?
Only the man clamped to his high-tension line
knows further into the known, electron to electron
sizzling in step, and into the peace just past them.
Ache compels the separations to plunge
rock deep, while the yoked contraries,
pitch with lumen, grow tighter. Yet where else
convene for the meeting? From the grape, gilded pulp
and blood's salty nectar through the ripped, given wall,
thus sheen sinking up the beach with spindrift,
yours into yours, mine through mine: thus the drum,
nothing for it, Boss, nothing you can do. Venus low in the east
writes vanguard through stripped hickories, in the Older Heaven
The Younger kindles.

71

When his arms jerk up, a puppet's
not in a V but catatonic H
head tucked, feet squarely planted
for the first goal in the game,
conspiringly the referee turns player,
black stripes on his white shirt galvanized
in the see-saw grant of finis to this trick and that,
each legitimate, none conclusive
in the long storm of blowouts, parchings, monster tides—
player against the very idea of clocks
rigidly ageless, solitary in the mêlée,
a Marxist and an alchemist—*Capital!*—in one clown suit
into air, into thin air
and *volatilize the fixed*
(soon settling into his vigilant slouch:
and fix the volatile):
no wonder that no side wants him on their team
for there is no siding with his Puritanic ambivalence,
ebullition and infarction in one dynamic
shall we say indispensable or shall we say abominable
with Milton's mein in a middleweight slim frame,
all energic states teetering, all phases razoring, into a paradise
walled and blossoming over longed-for reunions
under his cap shadowing a gaze seeingly blind.

Two

DENARIVS

squaring circles

1

Multiples of a decad spiral the climb,
ten proliferating the diaphanous-
gritty dirt-close stone
of the old diggers. Such my heading
in pig ignorance, it now ghosts Ktaadn-like
in fog or hangs bead-blue and tiny
in Plum Island sword grass. In the Mess, we feel
hungry only after gorging—even without *Zarathustra*
lugged in our kits: *Now I hear wolves,*
I must be famished. God the salving lesion
and balm if brewed end to end in ventricles,
out along blue lanes of the forearm
the all-mother of craziness and might
with the fluid zag of hawk tailing pheasant
through July's high boudoir, past the pin's point
as it homes. With one sound the sphere vanishes.
The climb is *into* the mountain:
that tip from the ghost Miwok tribe, cousins
to sherpas whose names I trip over: Tenzing Norgay,
Tashi Tenzing, Jamling Tenzing Norgay,
Nawang Gombu: four dragonflies tail to nose
on my clothesline as forty-one nations contest
their debt packages, two hearts parrying, pausing,
with metal hook-eyes bracketing its yawn,
wind swaying the razory white sag,
glinting wings high-wiring it
where I see that the grip I've maintained for fifty years
has turned my hands to chalk
trickling rippled crevasses to blue water.

2

What opens then bright, what closes then darkness?
Thus the *Tian Wen* riddled on our star,
through portages over three kingdoms
as across the Ninth Ward weeks afloat waiting for bus fare.
Maugham had his British doctor on the Yangtze
nail shut the well head against cholera,
then herd them upriver from the corpse field.
His cold wife warmed to him. He was gone in the next outbreak.
Swooning marsh grass the standards,
wind-torn melt ponds the advance.
Round tremendum out ahead of the column,
the button that slips every hole, neutron furnace
self-buoyed in the unbounded:
pretending to flare up then sink black, you
prop an unsleeping eye. Though life be
a wax fizz in your spasms, I rear images
at the same tempo as Pisanello
along clammy scaffolds at Avignon,
doing paladins who linger past the renegade
papas, epaulet and breastplate
breaching as gold from the wash of mind: plumes
and the gear gone, hanks of leather stirrup
crackled to tortoise legs cantilevering
their hold on the walls. Or they buoy as armored isles,
and I am the sea's now.
Vines redden their slope but no gleaners climb,
the far nestles within the near, deeps have
spread to serve as the underside of glare,
ease me out of this harness.

3

As well a goat song backed with blear silver
for tracking trampolinings of the waterbug:
skating on his folding lawnchair, he presses it in
like a can opener, holding all six thumbs
down the fret board of his string bass,
to destroy one city wide-eyed, then save another self-blinded,
Oedipus snared, agile on fouled heels,
Colonnus his two-worlded pond face.
From below, skeletal umbrella in sun flood,
rainbow feet dimpling iron filings of fate
through tears. On stilts hobbling, soaring,
the *sagax* picks and mucks his way across wisdom.
A mirrored pine spears rust mulls, thinking cloud,
its medicine the press of sliding dimensions.
I reach for my sketch of a bronze raised hand
to rebalance: Rome has pudged out its fingers,
sprouted mouse and lizard from the thumbs' hip,
set finch's head at pulse point and the garter's phallus
uncoiling up the palm's thigh,
tortoise inching the hand's heel toward Hermes
atop pinky and ring finger, flames from the others.
It is hard to maintain right size when auguries
explode the clock, to rest palm in lap and float
on the aorta's far drum, and yet
Ave, ave, this is your one chance now
to do all of us again, even at the pace
of hot metal sluicing, though not in a botched pour
into sand, no: right root, Vale, belovèd.

4

Sent his assistant
with his own gnarled staff
to lay it on the dead face.
But no breath came.
And so down the misty coast he reared himself as wide fire
flushing the Smokies, Berkshires, Presidentials,
spilling across Appalachia into the plains,
to press his bright hands onto its cold palms,
his mouth onto its mouth,
shin upon shin, and eyes onto its mort lids.
Finally a smoldering sparked in it somewhere.
And that was the first day.
And he went down again into muck and magma
and paced there, treading the placental
hours. Then climbed back and cranked the door
wide and flung himself anew
onto the limp form, mouth to mouth, splaying his weight
out to every edge of it,
down Pittsburgh gullies, over rumples past Omaha.
It wheezed and sneezed seven times,
it was the same and not the same, go tell its mother:
our Syrian policeman, our Egyptian screw.
And that was the last time that he would work that trick,
there were no more such templates in El's warehouse.
When chi and the void took up carving seacoasts,
they knew the crumbling outcome. Yet flame shoots straight up,
sic transit Elisha, sic transit what the white dogwood kindles
and the pink dogwood flares.
Straw bale, hay bale: both let us breathe,
but only one drops the seed.

5

Five-sided panicles of Mountain Laurel
deploy on the window from last night's blow, Stormer
Medousa, Stormer Odin unstemming them
from the far edges.
Each concave chevron of puckery linen
gullies to one spot of blood.
That blot cups the tip of a prong cleanly sprung,
ten of those radials from an erect handle,
satiny parasol tensed in full spread,
nylon, silver of the Gorgon head sack, three centimeters.
Out now and rolling: gone from the slung satchel
of wire braid and gold tassel, capital death he dared
snatch with sickle in his invisible mitt,
caput mortuum on the loose.
Peering into one creamed panicle, I stare into the puff
of a sky-diver's chute, his boots taking aim
at my mind, an M-16 strapped to his back. Something
vows to outwait him, bending over abrading
a lens: Archimedean, wily,
his hunkered peonage to soft rag stippled
with optical corrundums—
bring me my gust of platinum,
bring me my torn blossom, allusions
to works of darkness are not yet indictable
under the Gagging Acts, righteous hardpan
beneath my boots guzzles the torrent: it is
time to turn back-flips and gain the promontory
that has loomed behind, it seems, always—
unscalable but once there at eye-level—
and see leagues off into the last investment.

6

If menus at my corner café get revamped
monthly because necessity, declaring
law through pest, blight, drought, flood, crop futures, fire,
scripts my liberty, then daily the take from my dip
in blind black all-seeing spring
writes novum ahead of me in mimeograph
under scratched plastic near ice water.
Red Dot Special: between dot and spread,
the bindu and its red-shifting, bold-faced world,
between crimson and ermine, the gap stretches.
Yet the wavelength holds constant.
Where red puddles, its plosion and glow
holding the eye wide, no passport is hauled out
for identity checks. Through a manhole cover
propped across sunrise acetylene buds red,
and up travertine columns carnadine
first fruit, lifting joists, crowns as pulp.
Bullet holes, tracer furrows, sealing wax: farting scarlet
buses pierce the Paris and London of flung casements,
pavement shakes remembering its birth,
tars of the Pliocene sucking at cobbles, yet
who will not grasp after life even as it is?
Blinded Justice, her back bare
and her arm through her room's dusk
raising a fist, lorn, firm, even she
thinks her way past the oriflamme on gateposts
through a strew of gold and copper confetti
to the phalanxes out at sea,
their wind-torn advance creaming.
The praying is constant.

7

Same-sames along differentials, isotopes
notch the plasma exchange between
lapis and arbor. Or crystal lattice and grove.
Lapis arbor might be an engraved calling card
left on the hallway table
by the whole compact of the dead on a clear
midsummer morning. When I spot it, already the stairs
have poured my weight past the landing into
angled sun across floorboards
known in their shellac depth, but now delta,
the whole sub-raveling outward
easingly. Down each vein, that tree, and to rock.
Dirac thought he might separate U-235
from heavier U-238 either by spinning them
or varying temperature however
slightly across the chamber. That last bit overlaps
with my Father's process engineering
for a long second then dissolves: much closer
is the urgent botany of animate stone,
proven through disproof. Indonesian Maples
stay put, but the Sugar is a traveling man—
their bandwidths aching with heat, shine, convulsion.
Across decades I can make out the day
when a black stone, through one hour, pressed me flat
and went for the heart, as a not-yet-humming
X-ray cornea, its counter-weighted
bolt-hinged swing arm no longer jiggling, bears in
and hangs. But with a mind of lead that *graal*
pushing in with all the hurt I had ever
dealt out, it bored the wet layers, trued, constant.

8

Dirac, best since Newton at Cambridge, came to
Miami in age, and to *2001: A Space Odyssey*,
elated at seeing his dreams—especially
the relict astronaut stepping into an Augustan
bedroom. The domain where he had walked scout
now seemed a dead end. Whereas his romance
in young manhood, Lady Engineering,
that year got to the Moon. He stared at boot prints
on the grainy tube. Then thirteen downed on the Green
at Kent State—his Swiss father refused him food
when he botched his French at table… vomiting
then silent. Thus as Miami's president moved toward
the crowd that had burnt Nixon in effigy,
a thin elder walked up to him. *Are you afraid?*
Tell them what you think and listen to what they have to say.
The Grey Champion drawn from legend by Hawthorne
walked back into forest from the distressed settlement—
perhaps seventy, lending advice only
in emergencies. Now we know: his father
was a schoolmaster-linguist. His brother a suicide.
In the woods he found his way with symbols to anti-matter.
And to electrons that cannot remain point-beings
if they become string-ends. And what about
Nothing before the Bang? *That's not a meaningful*
question, which is the devout, not the rude, answer.
His previsioning of Strings gave him no ease.
All of the fathers want words,
while personal loyalty, and the shapes of true
things, feel true
in variables. Invariably. Alone.

9

Pouty gabbles of gulls de-fleaing plumage
on the spongy crowns of piles turn their backs on us
and on each other, Beckmann doing them in yellow spats
from bourse and brothel, their harbor patrol line
sinking then swirling back,
all the way from the Oligocene—
thus my sketchy doxology: hold to unseen standing waves
here though ungrasped, and therefore also hold
with Knightly while he plucks up the nerve
to criticize the lady
to whom he will finally propose:
squeeze into both the resolution phase of equations
and the dissolution apex of crevasse-leaps
between mental states. Or sing the curve not the intervals,
grant identity only to weaves among patterns,
for only then will the notes find you.
If you lose what you know, then in some other year
it memorized you, and
you stand unbound from the rack.
Above the gull's can-opener range the ripped can
trawls the flowing unseeking brightness so dark to us.
I sat my worst dilemma in damp Sant' Anselmo,
locking on twin dusky windows,
then on my empty-handedness, then looking up again—
where a third window hung, and bonkers it stayed:
so that years on, now, the news:
from dilemma to depth in one black dip
you won't take otherwise,
laving your agnosia
until what is not comes out of what is—whoosh, whoosh,
two circles interflexing, smooth same and dark other.

10

Newell Conyers Wyeth, in the canvas
that pictures a dream after he nearly died falling
from scaffolding for a bank mural in Trenton,
stands on more scaffolding, Washington nearly side-saddle
leaning over to narrate
the battle at the Brandywine, thumb back and high
to the action in folded dales under folded cloud—
that turf N. C.'s own farm, while little Andrew below
draws his own battle:
this brawl that shifted the capital,
the General outflanked and defeated—this becomes
the stabilizing clash, scarleting September trees
and blueing the time prism.
From shipwreck Hopkins hauled out urgency
Christ, come quickly! cold-forging his tradition,
Mallarmé dicing among the same timbers, while
Jew-spiting Luther pours his Ezekiel straight: the Almighty wants
a man who will shield men from the rest of God.
Early in late age shaken by recalling
the midnight Rome street where I stepped back to read
names on a moonlit plaque
when a rocketing car and its blast radio
missed me by a hand, I find not the required
candidate but a half-naked titan howling
newness in me, brawn streaming
green, silver, solar yellow, red. Thus the battle—
cobbles turning to raceway,
footing one moment millennial the next gone—
pours engagement down the time chute: this agonist
missing his left arm, mouth a series of Os

11

wrenching aperture around rawness, has nothing to do
with reenactments of the action
prior to Wyeth's misstep: he had relished that fuss,
20,000 watching the defeat two years
before the market crash. The slaveholding General's
cocked thumb, if it tallies anything,
does not stop with his losses but hooks through
the cloud quilt, its cream slashed
with violet opacity.
The dream to Wyeth: you & the banks & George
all fall but then win through.
Underfoot still stretches imagined planking
on stilts cross-bolted
through shadows, while one's own son
already at the same task
hunches at work on the ground.
Can there be more than
one life's infold in one lifetime?
The germ lines do not answer.
An ox's thorax my commander, neither
crazed Ajax nor Prometheus,
sums it down then starts from scratch
gurgling: the stub from one shoulder a caliper
aching to swing, it pre-publishes
the gut of courage
and amputated basso of all voice.
A bear's lopped referendum
to man, out of
all that was, reaching.
The stone, upon falling into the time we are.

12

And comes quickly, the stone, a fast horse called pain
to a stall fibered with veins.
Red cedar tendons out of dripping root fur:
this that I am and you are, but how shall we say it—
old-growth ribs waxing shaggy upward, mist
through its walls notwithstanding, it holds
thousand-old suns in mute cool percolation
vast, Titanic, and such as man never inhabits—
Thoreau soloing on Ktaadn
and found after my own hulk had found me:
I stand in awe of my body… so strange to me… What is this Titan
that has possession of me?… Think of the c o m m o n s e n s e!
Contact! Contact! W h o are we? W h e r e are we?
Paytaytequick is where, or Gribbell Isle, Princess Royal—
into the mixer poena maxima to peace,
footers of moss-shingled thalamos
as side to side swinging
a wedge-headed white bear claws at spawn-fat pinks
running slits up rapids,
white urs pinch-legged on ice-dimpled boulders tussling
black urs for a finny egg pouch—
white, or tarnished cream-silver, having at black,
the fight in that crucible known but how not call it
the immortal coil even from this thick intimation—
having known only one
ordained corner of it: amperage
pulsing in little space, 10,000 suns and *Tītήnoί*
cruising the punk rot of deciduous
devotion to receiving, in the one spot
allotted, the alternations, direct.

13

Productive capacity morphed into the leechdom
of absentees, and weaponeers on bloated
contract de-industrialized the remnant—
restive choristers squirm in their gowns, yet go on
further into betrayal.
Benda the unbending—*Julien*, Julius, Iunius—however many
might rise here, sunlit fog would snow them
into the drift, where loyalty is catastrophe.
For off-shoring placelessly marries nothing:
no rumpled bed linen, yet scads of brats
in private tutelage. My titan
could be gravel-mouthing prophecy,
but I know: his meaty ribcage and stump shoulder
tremble with the gargles
of balked life, mine in microcosm
of the macro facts. And mine the sonar pinging
off anything worth a spyglass: hic locus status nascendi,
here the one chance for amendment
even though embryonic. Whence sometimes in profile
a blip enlarges—the Salish Sea and chanting,
a prong prow, ten rowers in red, the steersman broad-brimmed,
perhaps the canoe from La Push
toward Port Gamble, many more coming, and I see
what pulled my gaze to them: at this distance,
millennia and side-on, their strokes
show only their left shoulders levering down.
The S'Klallam chief plants his talking stick in wave plash
as challenge and greeting. A cedar prow slurs sand,
burly nephews of druggies
and sons of suicides pulling their half-ton in.

14

Tiny Bath wears bowfront classicism—a plug C I T Y H A L L when Webster
went into the ground at Marshfield, his horses buried standing.
Close, the shipyard's 400-foot boom dangling
a truck-size pulleyhook.
Gravity is unforgiving, buoyancy immerses in flow.
When they lowered Yeshua in slings, those many hands
deposed an aeon's dead weight limply gymnastic
into altered perception. Rocking lightness.
Boatwrights in the Telephos frieze, Stanley Spencer's riveters at Port Clyde,
not here—yet life has hardly begun. The schooners
Apache, Nebula, Windflower in the timber and coal trades,
27 classes of cruiser & destroyer at Pearl, Sicily, Leyte Gulf,
Tonkin's *Maddox*, Tomahawks into Baghdad.
When I led young readers by tall windows
to kalokagathia—beauty&good—the idea had already
been decommissioned. Builders' models on restaurant walls,
gleaming laminates—I thrilled to those ships. Still do.
Yet their sea was Conrad's infinity frame around
our decompensations. A reciprocal whose prime matter batters
the Hermes-buoys, crapping our gizmos while
spindrifting them: suspended restoration.
Our senses, when we come to them, are not all that we come to.
Climbing a street from the harbor one glimpses
four-deck cross-sections dripping welders' sparks through
tied-off wiring from piping.
But cedar hand-carved, a crew heaving it in, one hundred keels
converging on Swinomish—
John Marin, Marsden Hartley, you blew light
into these ledges, firs, pines,
you heaved these rocks in the air but called no one home.

15

The schoolteacher on Monhegan, midwinter,
prepares as Jamie Wyeth saw her, a fork
in her open book, bare-breasted toweling hair,
the isle across-channel striped cadmium
with baby day. But she grants this hour to me,
tending the human future on its black patch,
the others sleeping, trusting she'll leave us room
to catch up, trudge in, then work face to face.
The lords temporal will not be coming. They have
the best boats, bodyguards in dark glasses
either side of the cabin.
But not to wooden desks with hinged tops,
not to school after sun-up. I too have done
her wedge of toast in mouth, the last part of the first meal
before the last sharp blow
of February, lopped month, leaper—
have seen her before but not tied the astringent
kerosene to blotted stars, purples in snow,
metal shaken in the channel.
Her vigilant slouch holds coming cognizance—
have felt it before but not pushed through wanhope
to willowy tungsten resolve
awake in nude duty. To trusting that she'll not
look up from her book just yet,
at most easing her belly a shade more toward
the half-lit curdled slope cupping a red truck
and a litter of roofs on basalt.
Those lords are determined. The end seems determined. But here,
absorption while transmitting: that milk,
mulling in flesh and the black flagon of all-might.

16

Mother of me you àre not, but the trail
breaks forward here, puffballs of breath at large
in the blown meshing spirals,
with a carpenter scoring each pass on the lathe.
And with the elements: your lessons go
to each limit then stop at the stretched
tangle of knowing with doing,
leaving the night to sink each knot. Africans pushed
by the Sahel and sizzled by wires
overhead in the Channel Tunnel—
word had reached them, they were bent on squeezing
into her room. A world each time
goes when a jammed barrier, bursting into
the next unimaginable phase, three
to four, four to five, makes fatality
not something other, but something otherwise
conceivable. Sun-and-salt-spray mummies
from Senegal on a boat bound for
the Canaries and Europe but adrift off Barbados,
they too had heard. Bread!
And now the greatest crime, with our boundary efforts
against it, to be braved, eyes open.
Yet if I saw her and not some wish, then I have seen
the five a.m. of the whole,
grammar prepped with the math, the lived hours more
solid for submitting to outline in pencil
by the soul there, filled from
plate and mug but also the bending far sources—
intent face at once found and lost
whited out by a returning beacon.

17

The malls, sheeted in plywood, lease promenades
that dwarf the Forum and the Arcades, to pods
of the feeble and mad: fountains, benches all theirs,
palatial toilets, chaperones unleashing them,
a bearish retarded gait under skylights.
But the prototype heaves a hooked forearm
through branching radials of system
toward the bulge, the sweet long sack.
Which sinks in with his lancing jab,
woolly buckshot whining from it.
The elongated skull drives in on racks of keyed firework
hoarded through the amnesiac year, until
philosophy finally hangs justified: the huge
anemone, pushed out through risk, the study
of dying consummated,
attains its chrysanthemum at total wattage,
the pallet of all colors
creaming down the dark.
Oaf, stealer of sweets, baggage handler,
muck dripped from the wheel,
sleep of aeons grown boned and furry,
make separation!—
to claim your seat at the last banquet
you must grasp my hand.
Tears, mass's cupped moiety,
the head cradled in both arms' wide pliers,
queen mantis on due reflection eating herself:
the bunghole through which one goes
will steady as Venus does at evening on the rim
of the second world, lamp over the other sea.

18

Not barreling fire cloud down the coulées,
but hanging into tendon burn; letting January rains
sag him along the trunk of cosmos—
this is Bear, and that's that, file the folders.
Yet he shot through Copenhagen on the express
hulking intent over his math, the acerbic
at times callous Pauli, and from later confirmations
of the precise moment of his passage
the assistants in Bohr's lab established
that once more the Pauli Effect had made their apparatus
go into twists. He, the only magus who refused
to work with Oppy on the Bomb.
Scrappy Oppy photographed later leaping,
turned from his blackboard
to catch chalk flung seconds ago—
stopped before theoretic explosion at the apogee,
suspended in creepy offertorium, selfsame into selfsame
with no drop into dread efficacy,
no touchdown countdown, a tetch less crazy
than when he herded Wunderkinder
in the desert, and no longer wilting at long tables
in the Senate grilling chamber. For at last
he hangs into the dreamed outflux of the small
into the brain of the large, talcum bloom
on its stem, shuttlecock not coming back.
For the one who sent it hurtling kicks wreckage
at the tree's base: skies and seas, leafy eras,
their gleaming stabilities jostled in the sway,
flung there for their self-outwearying lord,
self-voltaging bolt, the boss.

19

Nearly submerged in the mug, my spoon trails cyclones:
how far down into the steaming creamed
mocha flecked with chocolate can I drive
the steep swirl? Polar wind drags at the roof
as the sunk pocket gullies to swiveling gleam,
and for one gulp swung power lines dim
inner day, sucking at the hum,
a great thing hanging shy of the controls,
the sputtering generator kicking in
through influxes of an immeasurable swell.
Down to the oak windbreak and the bog's
ice-lacy skirt, as out over decades
of centuries, the cocktail-holding stances
of my former attitudes
obscure the hale dead and and veil with bouldery
massiveness my near-fatal illness,
having ears only for each other,
ignoring rupture with chumminess and slow fades.
Nicholas von Flüe, heartsick captain, paterfamilias
in his tight valley, the era of Jeanne d'Arc,
was pinned as if by his own sword
when a tall wanderer walked into his skull
and sang to him. And loved him.
Echo-imaging of the heart's action
shows it: mortars lobbing flame through blue draperies,
drumming white, yellow, orange,
all these pulsing the cornea
of the stranger. On him the bear shirt shone
the way a well-wiped sword sends
gleam bounding and scattering across the walls.

20

A throne flanked by two wolves benched the Stormer.
The fatherhood of known with unknown
sank piles for psalm and anthem, Latin against the North,
chancels against stave and bog. Came thence
unprecedented crimes. Yet mead hives a trace,
and you have to stay on it, the belly's fierce processes
going with it: how an illiterate magistrate and commander
abdicated to a tuneful wanderer in bear shirt, as if:
The sword of no sword! Mine, by the patience of long rule!
Mine, by the blade's interior halt and sheathing,
mine, by the leopard led in and couched.
For Swiss Nicholas, the keen sin of holiness
out of wolf haunches folded smoke, the urn throne
pouring itself out unto itself.
Ich bin analphabet, do you read me, do you read me,
Ursgodman is standing me down,
erect in blown fuses where it took form, connoisseur
of the two natures yet bent on squeezing
the comb haulers among runt humanity,
bung-holing them through themselves,
status spattering. The uncorked elites at their long tables
will hoist more wine from their drones into firelight,
yet those minds of blood, until and unless
mirrored in it, shall paint the sand.
Mine ghastly by the quaked film there, by the baritone gaze
decoupling me beyond all
expectation. *One of us*, mutters carbonic cumulus
as it spews charge, love gone strange
as it rears. Over its coat the coal chute of stars,
down its maw the red life.

21

Or fear for integrity, that claw unsheathed:
it swipes with sable arm, brunt paw—
as villager Jägerstädter left wife and daughters
in solo trek to the beheading dock, one man:
a medieval far ahead of me
to my scandal, farmer-Christer tormented
by terror of the horde within him, Wotan's
but as nation-lovers, newly greatest,
anointed to redeem
frustrated destiny, manifestly, in gut glory.
The bear in him, chilly berg, stood fast.
His mountain did not crack open like von Flüe's
on untruth, but hung a train shiny
with modernity coiling down its mass.
Stopping near him, it drew the crowd on board,
gliding them away.
Swaying Afghan matrons in blue gowns,
ursine ancient mams of the strict law,
I may not simply tuck into your wallow
to flee my strangeness and keep the soul 12th-century.
And this fellow abstractly swirling his cup:
does he stand here so as to block the exit
to his own thousands from Crescent City,
cars in Saint Bernard Parish stacked across the lanes,
Gretna's police pot-shotting the Connection Bridge
to deter refugees: is this
his last long-handled spoon? Wind high, and a barge
bashing the gapped levee:
Ah, he says, these maximize my chances.
The change that has to pile in, let it, but bottle
the whole shindy: cork up the bastards.

22

My sensing and its rain trail mute mist,
yet still the brush-laurel mountain
shoulder-high hulks for honey.
Hearing, touch, and smell see the same muck
where the immobile stream wept and traveled.
And all the bloodtuplets of crime as the same crime.
One mind is the sensing in that root
which carries me as it spreads five fingers of names.
From his chamber of the union,
lumbering into height, *urs* is ours:
nostril's intake flares around the entire
blare, tickle, and star scatter of winter jasmine.
When Feininger at fifty sat down
to write organ fugues as his hand painted them,
he conned the bear's unitary wandering
down the tree into the tones.
So that when Hornbostel told such stories in Berlin
to paint the oneness of sensing,
students in his honor danced on the Stube's long tables.
So that when Frederick Douglass
pushed his last sentence at the throng in Rochester,
the applause broke over him as both
praise and thrust: they had to push back,
yet his stance held. Again they piled on, and he held.
One terror with one sweetness go forth
from the paw's arc, as one force
in those whose fives jag to integrals,
and who, assaulted, remain themselves.
At counsel with the comb's drip,
stung, at stand, consolidated.

23

When I talk with you, I take counsel with myself—
thus Odin muttering through the whole era since
the popular saints of the 15th, nation builders Klaus & Joan—
Christ in their milk taming
the wrath they also aimed at, and with, a world—
while at the other end of that telephone
my silence hives swarms of babble.
Nine nights on the tree, then runes for that, their stone—
raise a child, write a book, plant an oak:
this still the measure for one span?
At three, shafts of sun bleaching newsprint
spread on the floor, I'd mouth the shapes of words
in the headlines, singing out stumpers toward the kitchen.
Selbstmord attempted in the house, Selbstmord on military service—
that family clutching to its side innocent hells
as the Spartan boy hugged his cloaked wolf cub
bleeding in the ranks, upright ephebe:
yet those codes were strings in the tree, sucked by sun
into the unbounded, while refugee letters
lumbered orange on night's rim, plowing vapors.
The half-life of a realization: I've juggled
the yarning stripe of some old kabir,
the breath and uot of push, becoming man
only through a swerve. *Uotan* they called
the switchman glint-eyed at joins of the rails. Long
drumming of the freights! Urs as otter, ripple-browing
crawdad chewer, bass-and-perch slitter, scholar
of downbeat architecture and upstream cuisine, were he alone
our granddaddy god of engineering! Yet through us
the elusive matter propels.

24

Hang on at the party!—the yeoman republics,
the mercantile deciduous empires, cults
threading them like the styles down flanks and breasts,
cascading the aureoles—this fuels morning,
searing down bole and stem, their sway systems:
thus no more resin for such fires. A wet face
and then stillness, these stay. The arrays
throng in their variations while it waits,
a sealed chamber, the thalamos, make-weight yet counterweight,
full there where it fills here, yet secret,
drawn no longer into clashing fulfillments
that have no end. The replete comb.
And as bathysphere plummeting past beryl
through cobalt—we catch the flares and jolts of coitus
but grasp nothing. Bridal's red room—
the inquiry into its bed, the raiment for it, all
the scholarship for the weave of such bedding,
these busily braid, while in ferociously
dumb fumbling the lords temporal tear at
what they construe as the doors.
A chief's wife tallied the Abenaki women she nursed
strapped to asylum gurneys in Harding's Vermont parish
sterilized by Justice Holmes. Told me
about the elder sisters and look-alike nieces
whom she visited. How the silence persisted. They too
found themselves at the party not wanting to be there.
No, dear lector, it is not you whom I nail, but myself.
There is one's lovelessness, and then there is grieving
for one's own unborn children: not enough
for those who came, and too much for the ungreeted.

25

Yet even so the room waits: fathering
cloud chamber, geyser sealed in camera,
fons increatus, lobbing jet of surcease,
bridal chamber, yours, mine, ours—
for the view from here, from here on out, is some
hired-on architect's only if I misplace that place.
For the point-rider of the horde
rummages my roof-tree,
holly prickles its paws among beaded hemoglobin,
and mastery cards raw flame,
it does not poke through ashes.
I invite myself to the party as a surprise guest
to carry my little room unafraid,
a gift beaker, and miss nothing, pouring from it,
for there is all of this to take in, while poison
percolates and sticks:
to spin what is deathless to spume, a heaved crest,
and topple through sensing into new sense,
tormentors turning into the tormented
once their crushed partners remove to that hologram
where crash folds in on deafness—
the dot-dash from fire in the open must turn
in the chamber to joined outcry, sound and void—
as the jar warms, the immured, married honey clarifies:
after the cranny the abyss,
after furry iron the gold breath,
but greatest, the inversions:
mucky abasement as sweat cooling the climb,
dawn blowing from the goal,
embers ripening in the babe's gaze.

26

And so it is no birthright,
meeting our clawed hulk as the melodious last
ambassador, but a twist as he rears,
bending as the tot's chair tilts so that
detainees must arch backward, blindfolded
into the baled balance of a dictated gravity
with the seeking, cracking spine.
To be convinced is to submit to conquest—
though necessity there wears shades and degrees
this side of a real giving-over,
everything construable as a show
if you so wish, as mutual enrichment
at the party. And from this unrolls the whole
tapestry of liberty. To hang, to choose from, yet
each of its strands has been pierced in, out, under—
for constantly a lance probes
the thalamos—bayonet
up through the bowl and its cull:
neutrons plunging a cell wall as the first cannons
had slammed brick and turf combinations
in the German towns—
or soundlessly in the castle
Helen Bamber found in the British Zone, '46,
drifting men castrated by X-ray:
the human hand swirls the beaker of night-day
smearing glows over snakes twining the god-staff,
and, auger-tip, my heart bores
into a cup whose hollow it can never encompass
though the ages yearn at its rim to con its juice and
hear down its sweep the suns ping and clash.

27

The new blank-windowed house will be lived in soon—
a scraper has rolled boulders and now scrabbles
backward, dust geysering from its blade—
might I back up far enough to shrink it
to a bee-loud chisel carving the iron-age
granite ball at Castlestrange,
those undecoded coils? (Soul
half-visible as body….) Pars inconnu.
Parsimony of interpretation, Magna
Carta of mind—the swirls of La Tène worship
rivering it in a pasture—
in terms not alien to a lizard brain's pedigree,
we'll soon enough want some Demosthenes
to pebble-mouth his gloss on us.
That bonker marble bigger than the rest
is a glassy sink for cream squiggles and curls
in the clink-chunk joust of capture and elimination,
losing or keeping all your marbles: his to englobe in one phrase
as a charm against Dark-Age feral Greece
by then legendary.
My house from here on out holds no tiles set
by my own hand, trimmed on a banshee wet saw,
grouted with thumb and little finger. The earth
sweating its foundation walls registers
nowhere on surveys. The oscillating
curves and eye-points on that ball
pasture the one-continuum, a field
a-swirl over granite through green unity—
a math past regret, hate, longing.
Once you find it, it rolls, you go seeking it.

28

Caput mortuum on the loose. The head dead,
cabbage in the last garden but rolling
by design: stopping it is, as they say, bootless.
To be planted, watered, Papageno tuning it—
all warble and fuss I was,
yet her one voicing went on past reply, stretching me courage.
Crisis was not about to break, or break some day.
The wave had gone over us—must we always construct the world
in the same way? Your haze
mutes riders dotting Poussin's peach-fuzz hills—
horns from one form of mind to another,
Medousa's scholars barging the tailings,
yet Tamina's cry—not on my vibraphone,
but high hammered steel. The kinships lost to your bairns—
those once-hived archives of meetings
in stilled glades and on storm ridges, forms hung
at pause, and cries held back as they stared or pealing out
as they sailed: these the encountered:
and all those never to be met, all on a wager
you cavalierly cast wide, with jet fuel torching—
she sang the lever clear through that.
When giving off light beside me—when her one word
poured etched, certain, as
pulls of the fates shooting white from cliffs,
then I could stand it. The animals
will return as swayings estranged, as she and he
were called, over raked edges shredding sans herald, incognito
even among Cedar poles
on the Charlottes, eyes, beaks, forepaws, dripping
shadows. Ten million generations.

29

Political animal—Aristotle—then *King Asine!*
that incantation by Seferis in my youth
at his reading pings out sonar: species dignity hangs
from one adjective, muting across snake eyes
repeated to mark full-bar pause, fat black fiat,
dotted bar fermata: will it breach now,
godly last playmate tunneling pressure zones
zöon politikē, Asinetē! Asinetē!
metals lacing the ooze
and just there schoolteacher Melville playing hooky
slipped hawser into disturbance:
The great flood gates swung open, and two and two there floated
into my inmost soul endless processions of the whale,
and midmost one grand hooded phantom
like a snow hill in the air.
Muscular cream mounding from rest, black dot flipping
white from long looking—
this too is the stone in augury, lapis exilis,
for watching it swim close one feels time stretching,
sirens wailing low past the horizon
as that back rolls and glistens—
thus the old ones came to stability: Sokrates
standing alert day and night, Ezekiel propped erect three times
slain in spirit, Gregory of Nyssa's Moses
running at rest in the limitless.
Press oil from that, ignite it in the parlor, and no longer
do you hear the language,
hunger is for nothing, satiety for nothing.
The dear hand, living as she sleeps, grazes
your pillow, but you have waked into distance.

30

Remorse the steady driver weaves lattices
through the lapis, moistening the joins:
ever building a body
purged of longing for escape velocity—
these boons, this weight distributed, pull down
against that instant misreading,
Michelangelo and Leonardo both doing
churches whose plans in section
double as Titan rockets, four chapels
as booster tanks for the last phase.
Just as no one thought to, or could conceive,
so Leonardo could only begin to read
cause and sequence in stones as given, *a book of the earth*
carried down by the waters to fill the abyss
for the shells, at a thousand braccia, were not carried there by the deluge
and *fftt* goes the circuit breaker, and it's high time.
It takes all of Kansas actually to think certain thoughts,
but the whole of the Trans-Caucasus to sharpen them.
Yet compunction detours
around even those, to work the pump handle
near the salt pits in the face. As clouds at sunset,
red-valleyed, magnetize the little clouds.
Playing dead for hours while hung by his chute
down the steeple in Église-Sainte-Marie,
John Steele had to squint at the fighting below
with the same attentiveness to danger, and the same
restraint from getting back into it, that I make out
now in the accruing crystal, and in myself
both fabricator & witness. The frozen drop
melts, planes default, a shear flares aurora.

31

Here: a flint messenger,
eyes shuttered, wears three sealed mouths.
Stone itself, held in mind long enough, is *angelos*.
Echelons there are, orders of these, hierarchies.
From the sea's bed, Purbeck
for centuries in rain.
Stone by itself is angel if attention sustains it.
Willing is useless among them, they speak of command.
Purbeck streaming yellow
in rain, from the sea's footers.
I'm sent to the back of the room.
Willing is a null field, for command is their speech.
Simply by being they ordain: marble and serpentine.
They have sent me to the back of the room.
Foraminifera billioned and baked, giallo antico.
For they ordain by entering being, marble and Purbeck Freestone.
History's fleets flutter over them and are gone,
billioned and baked foraminifera, jaune antique
in a bank or a pope's pillars, fountaining sound.
Fluttering overhead the long keels vanish.
Three faces have sustained me
but one great face knows me.
Through a pope's or a bank's pillars, sound fountains
housing me as I walk here remembered by that face.
Of all the faces that sustain me
one has known me
and flinted from it, eyes shuttered,
its messenger keeps three silences.
No walls now, I am housed because that face seals me.
Echelons there are, orders of these, hierarchies.

32

The grammar of assent parses
as in the '30s, by classes,
but still no general strike.
Codger Chuang-tzu by the drab square's fountain:
Work a lifetime, nothing to show for it,
worn thin, and what it was for still blank,
and we should pipe down?
They say Immortal, *but where is that?*
When the back stoops, the soul cracks:
this is to be celebrated?
Is life itself this dark, or am I alone in the dark?
Are not others in darkness too?
Crystallography remands no one to exploitation,
promoting putty while thinking diamond:
islands of sun on grass
through portholed foliage, the ocean from three miles up,
a veiled buzzing—
at that altitude, at night, a naval missile off Connecticut
obedient to its exercise
streaking in many eyes
severed the outbound airliner
and spread the evidence.
Mais ça n'existe pas.
If I can still see them, myself among them,
were we not…
there, their voices.
Not only begin with complexity but trust
its grotesquerie
to advance the fasting of the heart,
whatever must go—their faces, and memory of faces.

33

An elegy, northward, bubbles ores in my cauldron,
impurities black and zig-zag across
fume soup, while the squeezed people, spot-lit elsewhere,
rotate through, blips of notice.
But if you know them? The Society Page full-width married
a pair of their champions
in rag and sinew of poverty. *Don't ask us what we are!*
reared a tenor off-key and on-target
after Italy's muscled chapter. Ordinary injustice,
intimate, releases my own real devil
and then I know: I had intended to be human
but misprized the weight, the risk.
Smashing deadfall over boulders, I saw ground
rushing up and a rib snapped, the fat orange
of dayrise and dayset swung to a stay
through palings: now I was old and young,
tiny Job with the stink of Philoktetes
joining the war at last, hurled breath-tight past
the lead from Rome's smelters in Greenland's ice
to inhale Norway, stave-chapels hunching to spring,
pagodas steepling to dragons
through summer into blows of white wind, whipdrift.
Hip rafter, purlin, aisle strut, the fitted beams,
angel latecomers in resinous stagger-hatch lift.
Only the swallow hangs there, belly squirting shingle
then pumping steeply up her new chute, where reply
hinges and the sprint explodes. She, whom I now
release. For none of my people gave me to freedom.
Take to air, shackled spirits, it is past your time. It is my time.
Past north, far there, for me now a door opens.

34

At dusk in clover-tousled ground cover, ripples
re-zippering—there streaks the toad,
from immobilization vaulting through
an arc ten times his length.
Young Dr. Lifton freelanced out-take interviews in Hong Kong
with soldiers sprung from Chinese prisons, '54,
finding himself along with them *outside*,
he writes, *in history*, joining them
gropingly dissolving the grip of prior learnings,
theirs iron, his devoted. T h e r a p e u t
kneels to a discipline as to a god, while spasmodically
the toad studies groundlessness. Then came Chinese spavined
by the same rigors; he crammed on revolution, missions work,
Russian purges, Confucius. From bile and liver to marrow
in reaching the soul: medic Aristotle on drama.
Maniacal note-taking, tyro drive—then a French doctor
who quizzed him in turn: *Which side are you on,*
empire's or the people's? still cleaving to the clarity
of having been reborn. No longer outside.
There are moments when grass
unweaves overhead, light consolidates,
and I go there, everything as it should be,
ground still thrusting my feet. *Little Man*
so many have called him: half-and-half, warty
toxin sink, spring-cocked sidewall gazer,
warden of damps and sumps, back bencher then snap totalist,
Joe McCarthy or Andrew Jackson in old age.
bag of buckshot on a hiccup's leash,
magistrate then saltimbanque, the divorced
muscle of insight. Rumpled experiment.

35

In future a Berrigan priest, Jimmy Carroll
in knee pants skipped down corridors
in the new five-sided warwarren aiming at water fountains
past his reach, in age inscribing a study of that place
(where his father headed *Integrated Intelligence*)
meant to become a hospital.
Priesthood behind him, and still he, we, would get out of there—
Eminences!—but you alone know who you are—
may I petition that we be overheard
on this whole unspeakable matter? From loyalties
quite outcast, when all, all are disposable now.
As at Bezlan's school after the blast in the gym
that held the captives, windows blown,
when a girl of five, after clambering out
slowly crawled back in:
as the rescuer of her mother, or seeker
of comfort, or stewardess
of deranged parley, or dispenser of pity,
or bearer of *hostage*, shelter—
either the *brave infant of Saguntum*
back into the womb, or else she traversed
no known map yet was climbing right here:
allowing her destroyers to snuff her mystery
while drawing everyone, us together with the hostages,
into her illegible geste.
Some such imponderable power—
and children, imagine: in the quick
there are neither ordinations nor commissionings
but whale backs thrusting under them,
antinomian postulates, twenty twisty tons humming.

36

Immitigable suffering and real
evil, both off-limits to poetry
for Yeats of the séance and ceremonial
samurai blade swung in his chambers, he, senator—
and one of those was named *Contained Radiance*—
his vote weighs heavily. I grant him
his investiture and his verdict, renewing
my nod to the slight means that the unwound
spool of tungsten stretches before force,
its tension not a vaunt
but a dare and a tuning. Delegation, however:
that theme cuts close: a giving-over of authority
to minions trusted to speak past death.
Sappho's appalled cricket cage, tomb-loud and tomb-hollow.
Not as we let Leviathan kill in our names
singly and en masse, that giving-over
so immured in the reflexes that objectors
go shunned—but instead, as a billow at smash
up the beach hurls salt haze through suns, through beacons.
For those who dò kill in our names,
for those who refuse also, caliper arms nearly
touching where agony in quantum still gaps,
comes raw cry, earlier than lament
or the squalling pipes. A whole people wills it
but the doer stands shaking, it ends in him.
In 'Nam the 'copter pilot killed while ferrying a shithouse
lay under its wreck and mess,
the one signal to another man broken there
that let him say, *That's how I wanted to go.*
Moss agate blots itself, orphan lapis.

37

A whisper insinuates: what if you lived
from the beginning out along the bow
of the balcony, up on the balustrade
over the pit, the orchestra's machinations
visible, the paint and posturing
side-on self-clarifying, even though
the famishment and explosions were real—
what if you were in at the onset
of the divorce, feeling and freezing drawn out
without term, and you could have brazened through
their separation? The devil in all this
screens the minus of an ungraspable total
hinting perversely at grasp. Yet this that you are
lunges undeniably aimed in spite of reneging and slide—
this our body, as if
floating through hooped chancels of Romanesque
radiating from a dome under earth, the light
stone-colored—as if steadily
opening into the earth meant for it,
regenerate. For there what we were would turn
in on fire yet remain the columned fluidly
stable pulsing of the globed cell. Or as if
equipped with bell-jangling spear
where runners dodge wolves and thieves
nightlong past the Snow Range,
for that is what saves what we have not yet become
from longings to be what we are not, saves it
with sweaty pouches of letters, inky graphs
past the lakes, starry waters—as if in full spurt,
the butter-lathered hide and leathery feet of the alert heart.

38

The solid thing, congealing down the elastic
arc of a ratio, one to point-six-one-eight,
declares no victories. By percentage,
one or two at most tilts the balance,
despised increment. Act, flare, then
the hand resting again: thus builds the stone
invisibly—so that the curves webbing
a sunflower's face, or chambering a conch
with ballerina-bright Andromeda swirls
downstage, romance the odds.
One makes out the enormous drag only *en masse*
and squinting: Counter-Reform Spain and gold,
nuclear America and its bank book,
grinding galaxies strewing boulevards
haze-torched. Whereas in the domain
of the small, just this side of doing,
the percolation of focus
refuses to resolve even as it meshes
here, there, and there. Henry Adams'
references to himself in the third person
in *The Education* ping-ping away
at this bi-hemispheric double-back somie
to the front of the entire wedding procession,
the lattice in jell topaz
still threading on ahead, as when Margaret Mead told Lifton
to take his antiwar actions for victims' rights
to Franco's Spain (this in his dream), but he
dug in, dreading their police.
Yet Carlist-Baroque Spain paints our canvas, which she simply
walked through. She called to his next dimension.

39

Spain had gotten underway—
he was eight, perking to the talk
at his uncle's newsstand—
then he was eleven, Austria gone, Czechoslovakia,
and he read everything but remembered
the call *N u s a m u r a*
at the subway stair as he handed them
paper and racing form: *News Mirror*,
laboring out of the hole.
First the sound, then the inked pattern.
That was Noam Chomsky.
Winter days out of earth, lifting ozone
oil and breath puff with urine tang.
Psychiatrists, men from pilot farms
toward a mixed order of Jews and Arabs,
rabbinicals jabbing at politicals
through dangling magazines—whereas
in Pittsburgh hovering along tarp
slung from a coal burner
the cry hoarse or melodious
women in babushkas also,
nor should a mystery worth masticating
stay from the teeth of a good mind:
chestnut meat on a drum oven
reaching it on cold gusts, the black's litany
through pre-dawn cognition
Oh dee ol' roasters go soon Audio ergo sum
brake shoes sparking the trams
kingdoms falling the peoples jammed end-on
and then quiet: falling in place.

40

The demiurge's earbox
plays all the hit tunes but slots in codes
where *J e o v a s a n c t a u n u s*
was cover name for that master
of cosmic motions when probing
the guts of matter, Newton
in apprenticeship to gunks
with the hobby furnaces
of the agents of The Most Low
and thus under wraps devoutly:
a scribbled page under glass outs him,
alchemy straight on, its long line
out of Egypt staying coiled,
its mercury poisoning him.
Closer than companions
his subatomic Son of Man among potions
while unknowingly he conned
the ways of the nations
in seeing and handling each other
with a stick up behind his eyeball
making circles white *darke and coloured appear*
plainest when I continued to rub my eye with the bodkine.
Keynes bought his auctioned papers in job lots
while Franco got moving in Spain—
the last of the Babylonians and Sumerians
jetting fire in the prehistoric
blackboard warp-speed of our wizards,
Nablus, Jenin! Meggido
the archaeologists
have granted to you in whiteout.

41

Four, when I reached to stroke her slant stocking,
Why he's a little wolf! on that trolley. My nasal angelus for tobacco,
gleaned from the glowing radio, droned into space.
And eat them up he did in the mossed forest, slept thinly
in his lair, dreamed inky penances in toothless age.
Mill soot on window ledge by daybreak, pinky jet with one swipe.
Power thrusts inward on the long skid of threat
while care fights its way back. O doggy species, ears cocked, panting,
faithful to yelping dread, paura fidelis in twitching doze.
Better than momentum down the long cold leg *Technically sweet*
crooned Oppenheimer of the hot hand to the bomba. To use:
never quite decided and never really discussed.
Smeary slide down the cold bone of *Gonnadoit.*
General Groves intercepted the letter to Truman
from Szilard and team. Retching over their glow-pot
they coughed into his pocket. O puke not, ye sages, anything
not yet chewed through to its bile estuaries.
In your alleyways, Kyoto, the sun of reprieve.
In your marshaling yards, Pittsburgh, hoppers mounded
pressed by many suns to one swart glisten. *O bright hour delay.*
Mooning off into space, hand traveling soothe-a-doon
a morning flower cut down and wither'd in an hour.
A sergeant at Anzio, the ranking officer left on that field,
shrieked *Mother* and she woke near the slag dumps,
for one keen scanner is the ear for comeback love.
The former tank officer
who had Beckett as his patient
called it *O*, algebraic cloud around each real sooth
that comes on in to take suck.
Come in outen the blast, wee dearie, come on in, luv, come.

42

Cry out, and who would answer? Why, ourselves,
once the fabric gaps wide
and the tapestry twitters *Hurry, I'm shutting up shop!*
Swift place markers, fire-winged gabblers at every chink,
telegraphic for prompt antiphonals, alacritous bouncers,
the chashmalim have sliced through evening and there you sway,
dying yet dressed for festival, straw hat drifting streamers,
sandals among jigging children,
and I catch their grammars of goldfinch and warbler
as your eyes enter, Tifferet's favorite, although your hand
at your side pins my focus:
sun-warmed past the sash lifted by guardians,
lifeline darker at the root, then a fanning delta,
and I grasp it for leave-taking: you held each coming at its Hello,
releasing it only after it had uttered it uses—
so now my touch mines yours for ores in the dew of farewell,
Malcuth of passion full circle, again within hailing and bond,
opening gates after the gates have shut.
Yet Eisenstein aped the chashmalim, testing our skill
at entering into the wake of his *Battleship Potemkin*,
that spreading crowd mad for bread,
to stage the Bolshoy *Valkyrie* in Moscow.
The gate there rose strait, a mere eighteen months
straddling 1940.
His longing was not yours, Sister: he yearned
for an eighteen-speed gearbox, *a process that puts us*
into its very workings, not as a vegetable mass
but as the whole clan manning the whole thrust.
The arms of his troupe were to jut from foundation yet also pulse,
willed while surrendered.
                                        About the fuss over the Moscow Wagner,

43

Goebbels said: *They are dancing the Charleston on ice,*
the Stalin Pact whipping passports
in and out through the pre-invasion window.
That meeting was mounted in gauze and mascara
under ropey, lofty Yggdrasil
on the floodlit side of the question, What is it all for?
But under these elm naves, dying Sister,
the beeches' knees, armature of eld,
your eyes search mine yet also
swing, scanning the leafy speech of that place,
serrations whistling.
Only your hand anchors me
while the young, moving out under
coppery reaches, two phalanxes through dewfall grass,
thread dusk's fuzzy gateway
and the metamorphic sword, whirling,
mouths to them the passepartout, and they carol it back,
at time's speed ferrying us, Susannah,
Tifferet's own girl, loyalty's meridian.
Then falls the mute chashmal silentium,
poured-out magnum, and I remember:
hung high over sea, vaulting
azure over the azure
of stilled depth, one razory crease
unfolding them from each other,
I saw Morning Star and Star of Evening,
two fingers above the line
and the same swimming below, Star of the Sea,
love's bitter mother
nestling magma,

44

each other's mirrors, prime equilibrium
in the two fires among the two seas:
sisterly heats rocking,
those baking abysses your giving and your guard.
Beckoner! the realm you luckily leave flames then rusts,
its mouth a racket or crumbling in desert and beachhead,
cadencing roars into whispers.
Horse tons vaulting, wings of them peeling off, that is not it,
the German-Yank stab at entry misses the mouth,
horns and drums astray
although Proust hears them on the radio
and Coppola ramps them up on screen:
you would let it all pass,
Wagner is not Darrow's raven-talk
over the corpses, *eigu valkyrjur vals of kosti*, nor the wolf
mulling them on the Norse rune stone,
for wolf maw and raven beak are the thing itself,
valkyrjur, and though you'd have seen through that slit in being
you would have let others call back through it
in Paris under the biplanes
or flogging their sound crews through the paddies, for they hear
the shrill call and respond, Proust at the wireless
before the all-clear sounded, and in the Vietnam film
through amps beneath 'copter assaults, destiny
minced at that gateway. And forests crash entire.
Your hand I stroke for its muteness, so that when you fall still
then its valleys, oiled with my tears, will drip reparation
down crannies of the unsounded.
Kalon, Malcuth, Susannah, your touch rains
the ash-soft plumb line of meeting.

45

The renaissance double portrait
becomes triple in Titian, who halts a concert—
lute, clavichord, voice—
by having his tonsured cleric touch
a young noble's arm while dangling a fretboard,
the courtier or prince still touching the keys
as he turns to listen
and the singer looks past both men at us, her lips
faintly puckering,
plume on her velvet cap, inky eyes:
intimacy here embraces mountain blackness
down the gown of casually worn rank,
warmth and ease accede to triangulation,
manhood already models the Horsehead Nebula
in chambers, birthmark wart on one lip, so that
not justice in its acts but affinities adjusted
loft their dark matter,
and the androgynous woman
is resonance struck and fading yet already
en route back along back roads.
When after a weekend Herndon resumed
the Illinois Law Circuit,
he found Lincoln
still in their hotel room,
a toss of pages inked in three colors
with problem sets from Euclid:
Billy, I am trying to square the circle.
Thus Herndon knew it was not because of Mary
that Abe had stayed:
some other touch had turned him,

46

transgender everywhere through that moist quiet
before the town square,
the former flatboatman at times dip-rowing
with his three pens,
at others tilting back around
to thread his logic
with womanly bear-paw feeling
out the window. Real connection
suspends contraries
brimming to spill onward
through a barely sensed
omnipresent third:
thus warfare, and hale phantasms through gin-swirls
of squiggled struggle,
and the will either to pass deadly
into the cold porridge of sentiment
slugged into a bowl of crimes
or to heed one penetrating
touch through the clair-obscure
of well-worn shielding.
Even the filmmaker,
invested in playing to our corrupting civic attunement,
reverted to Titian by placing
the president's head at the same tilt
as the young telegrapher's
when they huddle behind hazed glass and oak frame,
their transcription cloud chamber
fronting the untenanted
desk of the sender tap-tap of the message, across
rain-streaked blackness.

47

One need not live on the edge to surrender,
nor sharpen the edge, innocence is enough:
his Russian Jewish mother wrapped him into her at age one
on the last stopping train through Germany
with one line-up along a field's edge
then back on: no recall of that, legendary,
with the difference that it was his ticket.
Such is eyeless stone, current splicing past it,
plaiting an alternate power.
Come, dear, you too are required yet need not speak:
ruffled papers as someone stamps them and The All twins just there
around chubby pre-memory.
Innocence your leaky tub puts out for an unharmed coast,
sky's unremembering cleanness pluming and wisping great topplers
neither piling welcome nor willing that you not come—
(In Berlin '45, Raucheisen pushed on
with recording *Die Winterreise* during air raids
He could transpose while sight-reading from a score set upside-down
and Claire Dux still weak from illness at her recital
but feeling his support, faked the high note, and everyone heard it,
and when one of the last lorries extracted them, he slept
unruffled on a plank: a good day's work)—
thus blue mounds in the eye—coom, wee bluebell, coom on o'er—
blau, wie im Himmel until body
held indefinitely pokes through just here
where arms go on opening: degrees of earth shelve out
that far, eminent degrees
from the Florentine's *little round threshing floor*
and Anaximander's smooth dime
ocean-fringed, sailing.

48

Just as what holds groups close
is heat rather than what
that heat welds,
so with faces
misty yet sharply recalled: they forego
releases
into high pastures,
from fears held tight in fists of virtue,
the clench of probity in good jaws—
thus at a reception for Gore Vidal,
the Academy, '79,
tall salon light in late Roman light: the old pair
had known the poet; at Yale their son had published
The Infamous while he lay in *the bughouse*,
the great tarnished. Below, the lit pull of Tiber
of murders. A red rose in his lapel
was home-grown, *James*
adores them! Waters thus tugged, mud-bright,
a confluence of themes, for the son
James of legend indulged
the breeding of orchids, recruiting and replanting
a friend of my friend—
thus it was that there the full twist of contact
turned my conchie's guts
toward the duty of fact: these were Angleton's
parents proud in their names, James *Hugh*
père of James *Jesus*,
with Carmen Moreno still a crisp duenna
Company woman: they my perceptual koan, no zazen
long enough for the job.

49

The bill of lading at tons where the heft came
to three red ounces
and behind them the night spring river
spread in spate just where Cocles at the bridge,
south of Gramsci's cell, had swung a sword
in mental fight.
The duty of fact sans the helium of afflatus:
reporting erect
in mud of the embankment while recalling
Wordsworth quietly double among the elites
of his long mind, one of them
his heart and the other the order
he had jettisoned—
espionage triage
in an undeclared world war, flexible
steel in an iron age.
Duty: he would write of duty
movingly, more so than the undoubled.
Angleton Senior loaned his private spies from National Cash Register
in Mexico and Italy
to Allen Dulles, and forged the chains
of the I. G. Farben/Chase Manhattan linkage
that brought in all the unprosecuteds to scrimmage
against the Russians. That short cavalry colonel
thus set splints for the tall son's leggy hybrids
in the damp potting soil of sequestration: glassed-in pruned-up
garden of forking paths,
slish the brute contact and messy wind,
slash the marionette theater
of by-names, inorganic fertilizer, double blinds.

50

No two hybrids the same,
excellence in the brew of one cup
drained without trace, inimitable yet sustainable
across decades and regimes.
Sic transit Angletown
through wet dims of the hothouse,
city that must be hid.
City that undid the hill by burrowing in it.
            Yet due to these unregistered
kings, an undeclared necessity seeks out
solidarity with the separate.
For their dark whirl
flings and urges only
itself; free, then, are those whom it disgorges—
thus I hang tight against G-forces that would tear me
out into the sail of myself, the sheet
flapping—I become small and sharp, slicing
into smearing onrushes, into fascinations with the allure
of tactics, of operations—
the flying monkeys are cooking my pork slivers
fish-style once more and
Were we fools then
or are we dishonest now?
Hazlitt our man.
And in the remembered sludge mirror of Tiber
myself peering past that couple to look for—what, whom?
Hawthorne's Monsieur Miroir *so imperfectly known—*
At Niagara, too, where I would gladly have forgotten both
myself and him…, my companion
in the smooth water on the verge of the cataract.

51

Into the duty *to* fact:
Edward Hoffman
then twenty-seven, a deaf-mute,
parked near Dealey Plaza
along the Stemmons Freeway
looking onto a railway span near
the Grassy Knoll.
Repeatedly
he saw *the suit man* cross to be near
the railroad man at a switch box,
for half an hour
studying them and the view,
taking in all its detail,
hearing nothing from the fast traffic. And then
the suit man at the fence
swung back from a smoke puff
and ran to the railroad man and
tossed a rifle
which the other broke down with a twist
and bagged,
running along the track,
the suit man
strolling near the fence,
showing I.D. to a cop
then mingling with the growing swarm
coming around said fence.
Half an hour of seeing,
uninterrupted,
honed by years
of unending silence.

52

Reports through more than a decade by those agents
who did not try to bribe or shush him
strewed cavalcades of errors.
My love, the Lebanon of your scent
is a garden enclosed, and you are
like unto it.
No hint of his attempts enters the Commission's record.
See where he stands—
behind our wall he looks in
at the window, he peers in
through the opening.
They tried to strong-arm his dying father.
Come then, my beloved, my dove,
hiding in clefts
of the rock, in coverts
of the cliff,
show me your face, let me hear your voice
for your voice is sweet and your face
comely.
Ed Hoffman, Man of the Courtyard,
of trellised vines
humming
with drones into late May
and primal sensing
crannied with pollens
of the open
before anything sang,
your gestures
weave and carve at the air
with one mind.

53

That whirl that smear that *underwood*: look at it without
hearing, *Guarda e passa*, go
right on by it?
For fifteen years the Pandavas
plot their revenge in the forest,
then arch-archer Arjuna freezes in the front rank, but *sees*, and goes
right on through with it?
I am the quantum *and* the wave, saith Krishna in 200,000 lines.
At that reception for Vidal,
after the improbable couple
it seemed that I still claimed voice,
yet out in dew-heavy grasses of the giardino
whereas was still twisting *whereof*
through *whereat*: evidence
stays mute
unless sifted against blackness
at full valence,
power known whole and fatally
as Kennedy's,
innocence knocking on doors to signal about it
as Hoffman's—
Unsäglich, o-
nuit-
sprechbar, ines-
primibile.
Thus into dark, the twelve
star months on your back,
lightless toil but real meeting as your enemy
clink-chinks your glass: go with jaw spiked to such mating
though not friendless.

54

Out of all such separated witnesses
rises one, his forefinger weaving the storm of multiple sclerosis,
one hand shoving something away while inviting it,
as he sets out an Irish tale he had taught at school:
how bastard Maíle Dúin's scrappy crew of sixty
hove up on horse-islands, the third nasty with more of the weather
that had kept Maíle Dúin
from working vengeance on the killer of his father,
Ailill the Edge of Battle. Our man's dad
had run U.S.A.I.D., A.I.D. also to certain other
agencies: noble and hateful to his son still, shaking—
that third island
rose fenced with stone, where a huge beast
tearing around it
shot to the heights, turning
upside-down, its muscles
and guts whirling
inside motionless skin, then the skin
for a long while eddying
slo-mo across stationary bones and guts,
and finally its lower body staying put
while the upper part spun
with the retarded
gutturals of a millstone.
And they ran.
And it hounded them, the rock it hurled
shredding Maíle's shield and drilling
into the keel of their
triple-skinned curragh.
My friend sat still.

55

Thus in obligation to the separated,
impossibly I would narrate the undeniable
in what they might have denied to the end, inscrutable
in some part even to themselves,
as Hoffman suffered the hurt
of both not hearing
and nearly going unheard. Saving hurt!
Thus this poem lays out spans at 6s & 7s with themselves
because I count cadence
to push past my own glottal stoppage—
remarked, it now seems, by Gore Vidal at the reception,
cutting me off every time I opened my mouth
then taking his leave sardonically:
De-lightful talking with you!
Scourge of his own class, belatedly now my tutor
gratefully acknowledged:
crossing that room from the Angletons to the klatch around him
has taken me thirty-five years, well past
his own passing: my aphasia then at aphelion
without infarct, thus now
I dress right on a Joseph born at West Point,
not dropped from that role scripted by his inheritance
but dropping himself
down that one hole in which
the sun vetted him and no other at high noon:
I owe him for getting me past gasping, at last pitching head-first
into the brand of astronomy
that dirties one's shirt but plants one's feet in Egypt
lonely as Walt en route from military hospital to rooming house
while at home with Then and Now and even You.

56

Even with widow X, my American-Swiss landlady
silenced by dementia, but not before the night
that sprawled her gauzy-gowned down the stair treads,
switching on a socialite's blue blinkies:
Now we'll just pretend that this didn't happen, won't we!
Close by the parlor where Dulles had fetched up for tea.
Where eminent refugees too had fetched up.
Silenced? A berg edging into sight, gulls circling it,
a blanched mountain meltward
the streaks on it clear wine,
Your hair is a flock surging down Gilead, your look
an army that will never turn back.
Parlor beams black with four centuries—
oh we have had Mr. Dulles for tea till it estranges
strangeness to tally;
have asked him about the piece on the shooting in *The Nation*
Really? cackling to packed seating, then disdain—
and about her old boss: did she put it together or pass over it
as did the Estates General?
The monster, the de-
monstra-tion, fishtails down in the cells
as their clear jell
pulses then stills.
Save me, rude health, save me with my own rot,
plant my black rod.
          Yet to that trickster-assassin I owe
nothing less than
initiation. Where one splits into two
number itself begins, states bud, fire explodes
to the pines yet unscathed.

57

Where wind shreds along heaved ridges
cloven forces clone themselves smaller, gowning in whites.
And person, tersely
breathing from gun or flower
splays its unity across
the same jattes upward accelerando
and strange grows the whole
lit familiar.
Steepling scatters of wind gust along basalt
to jet in plumes misting as one again—
and there is no passkey to these thermodynamics
of the unspeakable:
the hand I watched
twitch at his boutonnière was not graspable
even in hand-off to his offspring
drawing strings together
to cadge
asset Oswald and president
in one red smother,
a wilderness of mirrors
said James Jesus of his domain, reflecting Ezra's
broken bundle of mirrors—
dreaded are the peaks
yet comely the feet of those teetering there
still at one with themselves
past malignancy,
piercingly
tarrying: comely
their cloud scarf and its passing.

58

A gap-edged Roman denarius, late Republic,
hangs before me as mirror
of what and not who: columns in the background,
a helmed consul flanked by senators and tribunes,
he fingering the coils
in a cleavered bull to search out the event
while a bald haruspex
leans in to divine the auspices.
Bits have been chewed off: the tremendous head,
forelegs, the shanks of two swords, half the steps
and pediment; remaining, the armature
of a constitution sound in basis but
convened now in survivorship.
Now! how long will it take them to read it, and do
they have that kind of time?
Secret earth's naked dangle, hand lifting from
plucked strings, thus drawn forth the root shivers
and stills in hidden wind: totality
as the air spindled by cradle-cry,
the sleeve of coming forth by day sliding
that close, only thus its coolness.
You, yes, yourself here ungraspable,
all of the stories no longer at beck.
And in the damage a fresh evening knowledge,
the closest ones having crossed from hand's reach
already into luminosity—
pulse of the deep congregation, the walk
from here to there through bird chatter's vast room
accusing nothing, remanding no one to custody,
Martin, Johannes, Oscar, Carol, Ruth, Elisabeth.

59

The task smells sharper now. Hill-town dusk,
so much to inventory
in the last wash of orange:
iron rubbed smooth as silver in muscular
tiny crucifixions on a gate trellis, their backs turned,
and on a mound past it slung like a bronze tam
a helmeted woman rocketing a quadriga,
hooves pricking up clods.
No matter how I came at it,
that disk hung out of reach, low-relief of the still not
attained yet possible, in a gleam sliding off
dewfall grasses. As if the thing waited
for a mallet stroke. Leaving, Thoreau
whispered *Moose... Indians.* Following, then trackless.
Maybe sacking his rant at their hunt in *The Maine Woods*?
It is either universal bereavement
pinging with the momentary god in it
or a liner's deep hoot making port. And then
it was with us, our hour. We who had fumbled touch
were with each other, through cracked circles
in the blurred learning:
no oracles, chance still open and breathing,
and we swung toward midsummer morning.
Across the unmarked we fanned out
toward a windbreak of poplars
where an unidentifiable
carcass hung redly, the angular
choosy wrath of vultures
probing it. Who turned to the sun spreading wings,
drying them. Behind me, the companions.

60

Volcanic from uncounted suns, elements
brindle the blood cut loose like thousands of wolves
across tundra in Boltzmann's analogy
for the thrust of forces to their last scope—
the breaking of every trope, entropy.
Thus bulges the ruby
on the pectoral, manganese the red gate for mercy
and vitals, both. The science for this is young—
polar lakes, lovers in their beginnings
even on the rim of disaster hold it
on deposit: in their clear deeps dangle
ions of dawn freshness in ancient delay,
inexhaustible. Yet the man
watching one of the Pleiades streak down
and questioning his eyes and his mind, knows
that it follows from his own bungling—
ignorant of the tales
hung on them, he sweats dread,
but where is he?
In the back rooms of what happened
yet cannot be allowed to happen. Extinction,
but also forty new stars
that sprang out in Galileo's tube
when he trained it there: birth on birth.
With the lightness of post-whammy tritium
and the grind of steel boules with reverse spin
burrowing into sand,
the onward dark
raises the reveals to one man then the other
velveting melds that love would complete but mùst not.

61

Yet wait:
        time—when the allotted disc
already hangs chewed off in places,
or dinged, or dented—time seeps value.
Even so, deal nobly with time
and the tsunami will not vacuum your beach
but bathe your ankles, destroying nothing,
rinsing no single sense but threshing the basement
current through all of them.
A stream machine with no moving parts, the rimless
listening not yet in your ears but already
prayer's underpower, will be yours—
with the sightless all-directional mercury
at bulge in the images
while ebbing at the eye's corner: that too
pushes the velvety volumeless
undersense in sensing. There it goes,
a stern wheeler, two bowsmen dropping the leads:
armored, windowless, streaked by rust,
black boys chasing it,
it labors through the turns, high in the cabin
two beads that are human heads,
cinquecento rabbits, jeweled fleas, bounding onward,
stones chittering on the paddles.
So there it churns, separate.
Sound that breathed accompaniment for years
as of thighs parting grasses
rhythmically, now in the middle distance
trailing faint smoke and set
hardened by histories goes untouched by history
impelled, immediate, remote.

Three

CÆLVM

marching up-country

1

Calipers used by French foresters
for spanning trunks of walnut and oak
rise eight feet propped in a corner, their sides at mid-point
sprung like a queen truss and lashed
with gray steel, their curved tips on the floor
ballerina mantises.
Wiesel to Lifton on venturing through Shoah
to confront the doers: *You must not make one false step*—
as the bee, cell to cell building outward,
his nibbling forefoot the survivor of aeons
or Celtic swarms through dungeony oak shade
trundling their hive toward sun-point: what probability
travels on the toes of those tongs?—
by straddling elder thrusters scabbarded in birth callus
the slowest thought would wrestle root caelum,
deceleration the last study
though not as nose cone to nose cone in weightlessness.
To arrive first at measure
and only then at discord as task,
a snowshoe sieve for Virgilian tree farming,
nurture carried out as a military campaign
and rescue forensic—cool, late, lethal—
these pull the mind of heaven
taut across precision and swirled magma, both,
where clarity lives differently: by cunning,
deserved chance, and, as it seemed to our captive,
his unmerited good luck—Lücke, the way out, exeunt but
not omnes—he found himself able,
no yellow slashed down his bark—

2

thus Wiesel's fate calls out Lifton's calling
to step into the break
as the hands inserted into black gloves
on the sides of substance chambers in rad labs
or dosage warrens feel for their objects through rubber
impregnated with lead. Such the distance across which
grasp lets itself feel—
lets in every sense: porous, permitting while hindering,
as the sock lets the foot pull it ballooning
toward anabasis, homecoming inside-out.
Clarity's stained grandfather, mind without let,
chucks clarity under the chin, the boy feigning indifference—
as a mason pings the duomo's rib,
macigno, the stone sounding.
Caliper nibs squeeze a voltage arc shrinking brightest.
And for those hung there
that is thèir caliber—
as the Augsburg historian told how he pulled the drapes
and lay face down, coat tenting his head,
when from the Bahnhof that shamanistic voice
rasped and against his will he groaned *Yes* to its edicts.
For how are we absent when our own torque
is serenaded, ourselves the bridge, knees blurry
to footers of the in-between? Nor do the great honeyheads
lagered on shelves flanking
the blackout draperies, glistering there, displace
the point foragers. Finders of the comb will bless
the dead queens and wound themselves knowingly,
holding in attunement to the needle of homing
in the Mississippi of force.

3

Chopin's bowler is the bronze discus
of Prince Andrei's fixation on Bonaparte
splashing the earth it berths in,
and the frisbee that Princess Natasha hurls past
courage, black through happiness,
one gleaming arc tinkling frozen tears. It was also
the Coke, or Billycock, on the working man,
and Billy the Kid, and Bat Masterson,
and the Jew, and Chaplin the curl-shoe tramp,
and parties riding to hounds,
and Quechua women in the Andes. Kossuth, abdicating,
fled to London and New York, but the consumptive
virtuoso had already toured: wind-chill and fogs,
breathy damps in railway carriages, tiny hearths
in the hotels—more than six months from London
to Edinburgh then back, miasmas spotlighting
his final year, anno mirabilis of the revolutions
and revolution's rollback.
His last address at Number 4 St James Place, London
stood blocks from James Lock, hatmaker
by way of requisition from Bowler of Southwark
to Edward Coke, younger brother of the Earl of Leicester,
one year post mortem the composer.
His mounted gamekeepers kept hitting branches. The commission:
great strength and low profile.
Setting it on the pavement, Coke stomped on it
full-weight, to no effect. And on the seventh day he rested.
Bowler across-river, the Fourth Ballade seven years old,
keepers at a canter crouching over their saddles—
and Russia hands Hungary back to Austria:

4

every time is the end-times, drama bleeding
past the footlights only at the thin places.
The dialectic, painted red, ridiculed
as an instrument for navigating night fogs,
bequeaths none the less migration of the clerk's
black-domed curl-brimmed hat to the railwayman,
who prized its aerodynamic stability,
and to men panning for gold. Though not to the pleb composer
who had his go, too, before he went.
Hatless, however, when it came to the low-branching trees
of rotten cauliflower
between the ribs, which has me hacking as I write this:
coal in a steel city, my England.
Only a few passages by this master have I volleyed
over the net intact,
their curves fingering algebras of dwelling
mindful of distant thunder.
He needed no protection: his mount, tall in the withers,
would have laid him out anyway. For already
he had begun to slow down and do strange things
at the beginning,
as always he had done in his openings, but now
more concisely, choicely.
Three hours at a clip, Kossuth orating. But irresolute.
Putting brakes on the tempo: is that a clinging
or the foretaste of real divestment?
In slow motion, then, ever decelerating, even as the pace
quickens and figuration
filigrees the bowl of night: posting into trees at a gallop
to our gaze, to his, rubato.

5

The first infolding of an untruth
declares the entire lie. The first splatters
of March pour out the whole spring, it is
pointless to run hunkered through that drench,
it goes everywhere. The darting lie
splashes, but emotion that will not uncrumple,
atrophy that stays snarled and damp,
feel company coming and exhale
spaciously, stretching to their toes.
Goethe feigned amazement at the Mothers, oohing
and aahing over drinks served after dinner,
though his jest was in earnest:
the great matrices, egg shapes of event,
work away behind galactic bulkheads
set there as a kindness
to keep us from the weirdness they bear, the boundless
entirety of order on the move—
cavernously immaterial sorority
smoothing and folding banner lengths from bolts
of haze linen, smoke silk,
to swaddle the fresh mortal and shroud the husk.
The first snare drum brush stroke on waking
from the bough by the window skids their whole warehouse
down the ramp into day,
and the wonder is not that such berthing
steams off over its
shushing and slide through the whole basis,
but that such tonnage, traceless as the steady
rain of massless
muons, has shot through me.

6

It came in Bruckner's massive foursomes—a theme
that even I might work out in score,
a third movement lento cantabile
whose baritone would loft the Presbyterian hymn by Sophokles,
The peace of God, it is no peace / But strife closed in the sod,
and it held for minutes, motifs radioing in,
sun a taut spinnaker across windshield,
twenty acres a minute melting through it—
until I was twenty miles over the limit
and eased off. *Inanna the inane*
caroled a coed between classes at Columbia
when I came back to this country estranged
from its ways let alone from classrooms,
a brochure in her books blaring ***CAREER LADDERS INSTITUTE.***
That girl was not my girl, my girl
was pondering the rungs, lowering her grip
one to the next while dismantling them
with a view to null point then hovering back up through grief
(hands rubbing themselves, and I could not reach them)
thus back into immensity, not known until then as finite,
not to be saved simply as the will to live.
In twenty years we would have our Weimar Moment,
few descending the rungs
to confirm that devolution, fewer caring
that dismantled rungs, lashed together and lifted,
compose a bundle of sticks. Assyrian guilt—
it is worth her life to know that too—
a knowing that invites you
to lodge by the ripple's burble, and will show you
not what you long for—keep that—but longing as resistance.

7

Her little mouth widened across the globe of her face.
Could not let enough out, nor get enough else in.
The half-moon stage at Siracusa sinks through curves
while on their masks that slit stays open. Through it
Sophokles both laughs and gasps at our troubles.
We cannot say which but haul
for oxygen. Here it was lunch hour
in the pilot apartheid state, dusk
in Tal Afar, and her father hears no warning shots.
Pulling her tiny from the wreck, the patrol
lift puffy folds, a drape fabric
or re-sewn from a grandmother's dress: gauche roses
nearly as red as the splashes.
The producers swear the plot was not theirs, beadily their helmets
sear the scene white and snort *Jesus.*
At dusk in the Polish Woods above our house,
hemlocks over a spring trickling from pipes
in a stone grotto: those would be the coordinates
in space-time, though what came then arrives now,
past mash and moil of blockage. From left to right
at no more than twenty feet,
interested in something I could not see,
the prinked ruff on its hump a bison's tonnage through bramble
no longer beast but quid,
the no-longer father of a father's frame on his last bed
snapping branches,
a novum vaulting from itself
already past encounter. That is how it has managed
to free me, hoof into hemlock duff
as arrow's rip through a straw target, hay smell rising.

8

Not the small pillow between my legs woke me
with warm roundness, but my ram's horn
softly stiff in its high cunny.
At the June window screen, surf from three blocks off.
Even in great age it might flood this way,
cock hard, sound swaying and the night cool.
A stippled Balinese mask frothed the half dark, chin inward,
red gashes pointing its thrust.
This was not about the busyness of marriage or work,
but feeling without theme, the great bowl
slipping from what it holds to shape potency.
I stood into something still arriving:
not our usurers' freedom,
but hard with blood older than the hunters,
prior to the great pledges: family, clan, honor.
No hint, then, of the ending of *Wild Strawberries*,
when Bergman's old scholar, harsh father and wrecker,
after being tucked in by his maid
before Lund was to award him an honorary degree,
remembers: they are there
fishing a lake above the summer house, his parents,
he ten, they sturdy, mother's gingham dress
and the broad hat shading father's neck
both floating laundry fresh, and they turn, wave.
The salt-Kantian phrases   *out-in & there-here,*   *was-is & will-be*
have held for that old cuss tasting forgiveness
but now they bail no such balance,
neither as moon on the shining bay
nor on the blacktop curving past
the unseen range behind the hills in my mind:

9

titanic, more than human in my television,
the parents of this equilibrium
hold back from making me their child,
one squinting into dazzle, the other lapping her coifed head
on arms laced over her knees.
For the ancestors have been repaid:
what hovers here is neither the done, the doer, nor the dear
awareness of them both. I stood in the next room,
tidal surf exhaling no passport
mit ein schrifftle unter mein signet
the new thing heavy with seals: Dürer's account book
on the gate at Boppard crossing
confirming to Customs that he carried no saleables,
for in fact he had left his copperplate Apocalypse
with the bishop in Bamberg,
leaden swirls snailing mud through silver
for I stood in alertness yet beyond. For each thing filled its zone,
my mark resting nowhere on any of it.
Don't ask us to look into their eyes, the progenitors,
nor at the caravan treasury of their clutter
as you would into the eyes of lover or teacher:
all that has absorbed the chill which it denies
and half-smiles back through it, looking to one side.
Let the girl go, you are not her finder, nor the harbor
for her shadowed galleries. I stood,
a moth percolating its loopy sine wave
toward lampshade suns, and followed its track
with one way of seeing, the other holding me
at large in the miniscule, without scale,
the perishing cupped in the unmade.

10

A hail of nails, finishing nails, a bee swarm
day by day lifting and sailing
through rooms of a long house—whether I see them,
whether I feel their prickle and miniscule drag
or push on clouded while delusively
believing I'm in the clear,
that is my wraparound
when I come to a stand inside
my motion, when the motion I am in
as water browing a swimmer at crawl
rolling inside her stroke
is blood's temperature and smooths to a stand:
as at a wedding, foliating powers
flaking from scissors, tailoring some vast work
that a bright yet blinding lunge stitches strangely
past disasters, then hugely abandons
to floating suns: then the whole party watches
while each knows the core matter they carry,
holding it in trust for the next meeting,
that much farther past fooling themselves. In Vermeer,
in Pieter de Hooch, side rooms telescope
onto men talking business, while close at hand pings a chime.
As the open-air tomb which the world frames in its constancy,
the room that receives it.
Again they post you as sentinel, the lone drinker.
Start with your flow when you tell them how it sounded.
Report the drain-away, the drizzle off cliff
into the canyon, your unblinking attention.
Though they only stand there, they came many miles,
and though you wait, you'll be the first to move.

11

There comes a moment when everything stands still
and ripens. September grappa, Pavese's—
a duke in the Tirol threads passes after surrendering,
the flautist swabs out her silver, blankly alert:
fumes!—then it comes, an interval
that fuses space-out with birth, although
the marriage mulls in a wet darkness
feeding on clutter, the years, and forms
miniscule mattings to web the bud.
Parapets as the one shape power took, then left
for shapes more portable—refuge also to souls
framing their hymns… It all bulks through cloud,
wells and clawed privies airy cold.
Revulsion at this sequence, or retarded wonder,
puke on approaching the portcullis, or sing-song
recollections of the minstrels—
clamber between these, shoot for the blue!
Knowledge, though, of what is forming, that's not so simple.
Wanting to scan the agencies behind this tableau,
weed out the diehard hotheads from the sages—
yet through a chink I spot my
trim double, semi-professional in these affairs,
smoothly tuniced page to the lords of
transposition, certain that he can peer down
all those corridors in the codes and break them.
An actor leaned across a career to his playwright, trembling:
People do NOT know what they are like, but I can show them!—
huge Laughton in Los Angeles close as
Hal in Eastcheap, as far as ourselves.
And scattered clouds are swollen and ripe.

12

They have taken any knowledge of what is forming,
feeling for it stowed snug by the team in shifts,
into a long truck's high dark corner,
next to crated and cushioned vases.
My house has many munchkins! Or titans, the layout slippery.
Leasehold or mortgage, living grip or dead hand,
this or that judgment, *Ours*, I murmur,
south-facing parcel cool in summer.
The richness, amplitude of the dwelling, undisclosed:
warm as hair in its auburn sidefall,
coils of bannister in sunlight.
Ridges of the skull, tent struck in the waste
fold not so neatly as an intermediate
impression of the solid factor,
blood over snow, dung in the desert.
Passed back along the column, salient gesture,
hush of pause and crouch. Weapons at light port.
Lightnings from Devonian Augusts
flicker along the rim crackling.
Boys spray-paint headstones, prying at them through moonless
turns with crowbars, practicing twists of the spirit, crumbling
grammars of gift with rites of the left hand,
wrists and forearms in vibrato.
Drops to the basement through a sprung trap, cellars
themselves unbuilding downwards: these are
jolts homeward, bosses and rebels fudge them.
What had clanged still clangs, reality when sounding
does without buildings. What had been a job of work
jingles and fades out, scaffolding shaking
under the agora's painted friezes,

13

for civic air is a drum head, homelessness wets and tightens it.
What I wanted was to live in a day of tigers
and terribilità, though I didn't know that,
culs de sac rackety with voices
criss-crossing. That, that's architecture—
hutch for spirit webbed in tungsten moonlight
waiting for the butcher, dead-end brickwork a grimy
ladder for clambering to its eyrie,
cumulus sidewinding through a blue slot.
It's a new smell sailing along. And tobacco
has the tang of grappa.
Bundled at the curb, papers in string, directories.
Not there, the one last thing. Back in, re-thread the hallways,
stand there, not ready. Still, the god is
everywhere removing, rustling.
Blindness peeled back, deafness, confusion struck off,
the multitudinous and sleepwalked stare, the loss put by—
didn't those big men wrap them,
wasn't it simply these they came for?
But still the building goes on, pieces looking for a puzzle,
close to an ongoing sell-out, sober
revelry of the saboteurs. Watch them.
Towering over the van, smudges boil
along an incoming front, steep as in the throats
of dahlias red-black in the garden,
abandoned. They can watch, and I can,
rolling fingers in the sockets where these orbs
translated frequencies, inverted patterns. Rest,
remember. Never the dulled excitements.
Touch has not been so costly, ever.

14

At steel-cut thread's end, frazzled measure begins—
at the woolly radiation off its stump
smelling of camphor and turpentine on a trunk laid out
on a ledge beside rapids,
sun-shredded like the best Cuban leaf
where the connoisseur has bitten it off
but not yet lit it. There sprouts metric, as when
a seamstress or sail maker moistens
a shattered strand with a sleeve of spit and noddles it
through a shiny tear shape or the tarnished
crimp-shouldered grommet—there commences
yoking and yoga. Which trembles on out
into the mid-October defenestration
of milkweed: that gray Art Deco pod
not in warmth but chilly sobriety lifts its
curled lip over creaming baleen
and spill-hangs the bale, for which Britain free of slaves
none the less was half-ready
to sell itself. Froth at the fall's foot,
inscrutably fuming act, here bemedalled
with oblong badges of blood cresting out of
its own uncarded heart: good seed's gush,
as Swedenborg, horny as a ram, Minister
of Mines whose dreams poured him
confinements and liberations in the sock-like-
into-and-out-of pulse of growth, tasted *heavenly living*
both blind and seeing, yanked out through himself
into, into. So it is, sharp imposition
and flaw; I would not have imagined how such unfettering
from behind binds and guides me.

15

The tally of atrocity, shock shame, pathlessness,
even the altarpiece painters
got it in. Whence Edgar Ende stood up from the family table:
I am going to make sketches now,
and drew the blackout curtains
and lay down over the cross-hairs,
the Nazizeit and Hiroshimazeit
and the porky years of forgetting.
Knowing how I got here comes only from the receding
sheeny curl of the rails.
Don't know who's driving, and there have been no stops.
One photo, however, I can read:
that face, and the potter's shed along Aurelian's wall
and Urban the Eighth's, roof tiles
out over brick pylons over
umbrella pines in the Academy garden. Roma.
They bricked in half of it as the writer's cubby,
with a cot though with no heat
until I got it up there, electric and spasmodic.
By then it was gone, the foot-spun potter's wheel,
but here it is, a disc for wet clay and then
the circular footplate—Athene's patent, alright, but it is
Ralph Ellison straddling
the beam-seat, his portable centered where the clay rose,
shoes easy on the plate.
Dusty grass declares June. A cigarette assigns his lips
to expectancy, a cream collar flares
over pin-stripe lapels, one hand
rears at arpeggio rest,
eyes shuttered.

16

No splats flower the footplate, no crud slice:
a page aslant in the portable is drying,
twists of weed singe
dangling wrapper, fragrant. Mystery in its eyelessness
is drying through the long storm.
Behind blinds fringed with moist cilia
he will still look for it, the second book
that is forming right there
but must yet go through a house fire
and be reconjured, staying unfinished:
revivalist Daddy Hickman telling how
he spilled from the coffin, a rag doll
clutching bear and white Bible, pounced on
by a red-haired white woman, six black women
wrestling him away,
Women just ain't gentlemen
allowed the Reverend. *Nulla die sine linea,*
no day without its line.
                    From the garden I dug marble shards,
settling them by the shed door, Apollo's false teeth.
The cell I was never assigned,
an untested conchie,
was booked through Hotel Irony
by the angel of death.
This man fought first with himself and a condition:
not in a Jim Crow army (his call),
and not with trumpet in the Navy Band (their call),
brewing his coffee with lab filters at room temperature
then heating it shy of the boil, flask within flask,
two decades later lecturing at West Point on hazing
as a lens for scoping out power. Eye hath not seen nor ear heard.

17

And closed eyes may frame second or third comings:
looking out into a cadet audience,
not at writer-curators and faux-shaman literati,
but from his own sociologies of riot, jazz and blues, folklore,
from cooking on convoyed freighters,
from hitching freight trains to college.
From seven months stranded in Dayton—
his mother's funeral—
cadging sleep with his brother
in a car at eight below, sherlocking
the doctor who let her die
and stumping for intervention against Franco:
then, there, the first meld.
At the mobile focus of rampage, thus night-vision,
out onto terror mundi and splendor solis
above the tram tracks—
put away your brochures, brother conchie,
I want to hear this man—
for where a rag doll spills stuffing, the symbol drops
its bags on the threshold, daring the only grip
on something that no one contrives.
Thrusting the wheel, Greek ankles one would like to ogle
blur their perpetual kick start to culture: she is no
gentleman, that woman.
Guild entrance demands its mouthful of blood—
keep pushing into complexity,
its simmer unmooring the garden
into heat ripple,
and no longer will you hug the relic defense wall,
your spit will grease the wheel and fuss the destroyers.

18

Life: *mine*, as we say, and I say it, but the chit
floats on linen near silver embossed by the management,
jovial groups or beached Crusoes
vacating or settling in:
janglings as close as Parry's Homer
or as far as Puvis' Romans, whom he too
had brought close. Only the sudden jabs
of my cold sharp wrongs to others, steelies with spikes
zapping in like the tarnished
upholstery tacks paralleling my thighs,
nail me to my one-continuum—
loneliness the can-opener of hearts
is not it this time but an old photo, mindfresh:
an unsmiling four-year-old blonde evacuee
at a railway siding barefoot,
her patch free of gravel.
Doing away with substitutes for unremitting sunrise,
it holds her small and gone anew
steady in the mind of after-blast.
Heavenly body, one flung ember as Aetna,
one salt-stung eye as Empedokles, wakened and not good,
raw and not right, no flights
to blue latency, the Aegean's shelving floor—
if she pierces the back of the clock to stand here
intact past K-2
in hair from the solar furnace, she lands
not only in tinkling thermopanes but past
quick incitements to gulp or cry out,
unveiling her emotionless arrays,
black light as brightness, and declares war.

19

Chocolate jellybean deer scat, fifteen or twenty
in a tight offering, confirm Thucydides—
migrations, wars, sheer bread he dubs as the shapers
of our condition, not high breakouts in thinking
along the cliff walk of words.
First, uprooted Benjamin: *the immense labor*
set us by fading things, their heap of secret resistances!
then unblinking Robert Moses
on his Mississippi Summer, '64:
You're working your way through levels of opposition (in them, in us),
linked mentors of shock-drift then shock-shift:
so is it irrelevance to secure a clearing
admitting wind and rain on even terms
and the next soul coming, and the event?
Wintry tussle then summer struggle
already stand answerable
in the limitless expanse of psukhē—
neither fool nor plebe to whatever forces. Storm-tossed pines
tossing the clearing, a green swaying scarp
through hours, work toward neither innocence
nor complicity but mime those sieves
that would sort me out.
So down the levels, through heaps: not flailing, not crying out.
In Gandhi's fast to near-death
during the Calcutta troubles, to a father who killed
a boy to avenge the murder of his own son,
he whispered hoarsely: *I know a way out of hell.*
Young, blinkered, I poked at the primordial—
one edge of it
poking through from the unknowing without end.

20

Mild sea sickness pours day-long
from the lack more than my own, churnings of bitched
capacity. For Skywalker's arrow
hauled from Mongolian Altai to Pythagoras
opened the best that we are, hazed now by lucre
plexed with impoverishments—
well before Pindar its day-rise budded in caves,
while now as slitter and finisher
it razors evening land
as finely crazed porcelain at a state banquet.
When I bought two round-trip tickets
from Brig to the high valley town, our aim was simply the climb
and a corridor window down,
our heads out like children against orders, leaning red coaches
squealing against the turns. For once she had not
memorized the timetable as cleanly
as the declensions she still knew twenty years on
from Pindar's Chiron. End of the line—
a stone-roofed chapel, and we opened the book:
three minutes until the next train. Which was the same train
and conductor: *Why not stay at least for a coffee!*
Staying was not the point, it was the getting-there,
disciples of Rashid al-Din, world historian
casting his line, rewinding, casting.
We hang out the window on the other side
through firs, bouldery cuts. The coach empty,
seats matte green vinyl,
baking through rain-stained glass, and I turn
and just catch him, sun sitting there green and still.

21

That has become something of a practice:
the one who is with me at all times now claims more of his due.
And since you are not here, I cannot tell you
how the two Pindar scholars, one in a Paris hotel and the other
coming in on the local, were to meet.
It was my idea: the owner in her tiny lobby
was to ring us in the first man's room
when the second asked for us. Number two is rocking his leg
on a silk-cushioned settee. We will be down,
she has replaced the telephone for the fourth time.
Yet she never called—we tested the connection after Pindar Two
left angrily and Pindar One went down to investigate.
Pindar Two is on the local back out of the Gare du Nord,
drab flats shining and peeling from his lenses.
The debate that would have oiled the hinge of process,
as to which came first in their long partnership,
wind or rain—Pindar voted for rain—still hangs over the settee,
stripy maroon and butterscotch. In the suburbs
Tsvetaeva reworked love letters to her Berlin publisher
who had cooled toward her: planing them into French, retooling
his hand to smother it in the new vocabulary, violet-brown
Borscht jelling on her stove
when I was so close to you on that random-bench....
The meetings depend on precision.
At your desk by the window you sat through the morning
turning German entries on Greek myths into handbook English
then straightening in a spasm: *Incest and murder!*
Fratricide, matricide, parricide, murder and incest!
And no telling which came first.
The work was there for both of us, ill-paid but constant.

22

From which we broke into the Grisons, a cobalt lake picnic, turning back
directly, our hostess having warned us
about the cold. In fact from her house she runs toward us:
Russia has fallen! Too late to alert the telegrapher on the express
taking Tsvetaeva there for her son's sake,
true to her rebuke of writers who went with history
rather than against it. Rashid al-Din shifts his bony arse
on the chair cushion, and one more khan
stands installed at court. They sliced Rashid's Jewish head off
a decade after Dante fled Florence. Came the wind.
Meetings are where all the real living is, says Buber looking up
from his timetable and clicking the ticket punch
six times in rapid succession.
I see that her keenness with schedules and grammar,
although it went with us those years, also occupied
a cubby in first-class, no one else there, sun blue on its plush—
no green vinyl. It steeps warming over the roar.
Came the rain though the Pindars never had it out,
whether rain running before the wind
or rain lipping and smothering the wind's hand
only sun on the settee knows.
And now the birth rate falls in Detroit and Seattle
as it did for the Soviets before their collapse.
There is greeting in hot unmakings held at no distance.
There is peace in the solid hot pour
back from the window's gusts
onto the green seat that waits for her
before her blown hair pulls back in and resettles,
Chiron's mane agile, mortal,
immortal teacher teacher of the heroes.

23

Praises and raspings—bitching with requisite edge
while caroling to the honeyheads
for balm-dripping law: I get the tune and the measure
but veer off-rhythm
inside such amplitude, even as its
panoramic grasp
sweats a vomited clarity in me, a citrus tang
wellspring pooled in exhaustion.
I may not be Polish but I speak my own kind of ketman.
All viriginals may be harpsichords, but not all
harpsichords are virginal.
Eulogy stitched into execration, lauds sailing antiphonal
to the nailed charge while the profiled eye
in its bone house, laid back in summer grass,
pale floaters squirming in vitreous humor,
tugs at red cords lashing its float, a Montgolfier
over Paris crowds.
As if innocent, that replete eater of light.
They knew, Menippus, Swift, and Melville, that the view
from balloonings off the whorehouse floor
swirls acid and base alike
douching their, your, my knobs, hinges, gussets,
gerd percolating
the pipes in storm aftermath,
no downspout plinking cool dregs of rain—these
the menu duly annotates
as aereated bile and clear puke from enduring
the conversation with one's entrails
while footing it through the raven's head. Inmost
yet of this very time: that is meet.

24

Freeman Dyson tallying stats for 5 Bomber Group,
Vice Air Marshall Graham Cochrane's boys,
read him the counter-intuitive results:
survival rate did not in fact correlate
with team melding and the refined skills due to
accumulated missions. Cochrane advocated
stripping a black Lancaster of its gun turrets,
painting it white, and jacking it past the old ceiling
in bright day to outrun the fighters.
The crews and brass laughed at him.
The word I'd like to get to you, fetching it
from the abyss kitty and dangling it in wink stillness,
would still be manned by hunches in cracked leather
past the saving, sweated idea,
downed over Ploesti. Forensics are dispensed with
by time and the star: the unsolved Cambridge Springs murder
in my school years was nowhere in mind when I moved
to Magnolia-Gloucester, the same when I left for Connecticut,
yet the hardware owner who sold me nails, the killer of homely
bank teller Doris Hatch, left her teeth in a Connecticut
woodlot, and in Magnolia a note for his wife,
ending it at the seawall.
Mist and wave sound two blocks away
loosen the armadillo joins of intuition, drainpipe elbows
fold over its elemental stumps, mercury moons
bead its hide, turnbuckles easing at the wrinkled
oil sumps of the eye ports, their silky meniscus a clattering
storefront drop screen, rumpled rumbled padlocked.
Inland the oaks drip Joukowski airfoils through duff matting:
like Hawking's cosmos psukhē plunges boundaryless.

25

Not Thames-side at the Millennium Wheel, travelers
snaking to buckets on the London Eye,
but skin striped with polyester in sun splash,
Crescent or Gray or Magnolia Beach, the maps vying.
On New Year's night combers foam
under googly-eyed freighters facing
a shore-road estate floating its television
five feet from floor to curtains.
The morning General Store suckles pick-up trucks
idling in a thimble circle,
storm-blown sand strewing cloud
through a blue rim embossed **CALDWELL*BOSTON**
its pavement moon puddled with runoff
waiting for a fire hose while kissing
tire treads and bare feet.
For weeks after the Twin Towers blew poofs
deck after deck downward faster than collapse,
legible to demolition engineers—
the unswaying fall also—
no contrails roofed the Bay
and three freighters stalled in the far approach track,
their bowels tight with crates in mort float,
running lights a two-color braille, life a practice moored
throbbing in a death practice:
Herakleitos signals that he too
stood where the vacuum hose sucks everything in
and tornadoes it out on command,
from a black window one gauze curtain puffs out
and the sleeper, thymus spongy with gamma rays,
will come down late for breakfast.

26

Here my shovel into under-earth, not as Galileo
roofed Dante's Hell with a scaled-up rock ceiling,
aghast at seeing too late that it would collapse
and trying to bury the error (though he got his professorship),
but no: five hotels on this Point, and when Eisenhower
franked the bombing plan for Russia and China,
secretly horrified, firestorm effects still untallied,
the Hesperus, Aborn, Crescent Beach, Oceanside, and Grand
lay in bricks, iron twists, and cinder gleam.
Souza conducted twenty pepped-up locals
over the porte cochère at the Oceanside each summer,
hundreds on the verandas, in the road,
and Hildegarde Hartt worked the rooms there,
nursing in France in '17, but not before she saw a white mass
in fog off the Point,
The *Kronprinzessin Cecilie*, sliding from Halifax
to internment, fog out of which Major Douglas MacArthur
strode before her one morning.
And a block of flats burned there before the Towers,
hoses down to the beach, nozzles craning off ladders,
ash within ash: as Father labored under Oppy
so Gilgamesh crouched inside Izdubar, a shadow
tilting from chicken-track tablets held end-on into sunlight.
Lost his side-kick, cut poles for the barge crossing,
drowsed, botched his grip on the immortal leaf-cutting.
And matey fails him, stuck in the Beyond transmitting
scratchy reports on a wireless
about a pale mass looming over rocks,
a dog floating the hand of a samurai
into the lens laid gutter-level, Kurosawa.

27

Before Sullivan, builders
learned to scale things upward without the ensemble
crashing through itself. But learned by thumb:
in the unbounded field
of contest, Pindar's oiled palaestra,
the science of materials veils the scalars
jutting through spirit. Onstage murder fascinates
while arenas behind the eyes
lay the sand, sunned mica spun
braiding out into a delta's loot-drops,
spun microns drifting tons.
Jacob's tribe made do with a tent in the waste,
a people given to hearing things
and so spurning images,
Elijah down to his minimal kit
meeting the whirlwind, and then the blast,
and then the quake, and then he heard it,
a thin veneer of no-voice
talking to him. That was well into the kings, the builders.
Plato against Dodona's priests and Egypt,
Sokrates lifting his poisoned foot like the Vedic swan
at lift-off: trionfo then triage,
rescue crossed by relegation, hymns by execrations,
acolytes then resisters, anthems on deck in running seas
while Bede Griffiths bends over finger in sand: *Soon enough*
the choice, adoration or extinction.
From Magnolia Point the Dry Salvages tremble unintended
breakwater through blaze,
aborted harbor,
spew of the old rock schooners.

28

Suffering tars in *the raven's head*—
where Dorn and the heretic alchemists
corrected for the long tilt skyward
by refathering the Son's validity
in matter, piled rings of the velodrome
cupped in roaring bleachers go silent
behind aching eyes. None the less, to beakers,
circuit breakers, the quest. And into Pauli's
dream of a world clock, eternity disking through time
in a 4-D rig on the back of a Mach-3 raven:
black for informing Apollo that his girl cheats,
and if Pauli went near your lab
it went hand-to-mouth at the Hatter's tea party,
nothing immune to his size: *the conscience of physics*,
although psyche's prodding him to lay out to colleagues
her tracks through their domain
he shrank from. The reef toward Kettle's Island
was a cattle-herding crone's
who pushed her daughter off a cliff in a Nor'easter.
Surf shrank that pasture where the shoal darkens
under fiberglass skimmers gunning it, their pert noses high.
Frank Davis's parents ran the twin lights on Thatcher Island
past the Salvages, the boy bucketing oil
when empties came down. Cow and chairs in tow
when they left for Rockport, his father
felt the pull slacken and turned to see only
bright spoonings dishing the wake.
And the raven's beak razored
Surhabi, the wish-fulfilling teat, horns dripping,
Athumbla dripping white for Ymir.

29

The moon's commissioning is the sun's penance,
the Luna I guard collars in a blue gasket
the smotherings of wild mind in a stopped gusher.
A cross at Rafe's Chasm marking a girl
taken by the bore sights on a rock
that snagged the *Hesperus*, gone the captain's daughter.
Young Longfellow stayed up late with the start on his ballad,
dozed, then sprinted to the tape, 3 a.m.
Windows survey the Woe
from the Gothic keep that John Hayes Hammond piled up
with spoils from Belgium's battlefields,
lab where he cobbled radio control for ships, planes, torpedoes,
remotely aimed hypoxia swimmers, while Garbo in his pool
practiced the almond-eyed backstroke.
Nor is she to blame, nor Hathor-Sekhmet,
hooves jubilant in the hoe-down
trampling mannunkind for its plot to bump off Re
who none the less poured out wine vats, decoying her.
A soaked ruminant does not browse by night,
intellectuals chewing from nose-bags have no excuses, they are
cut adrift at the stern.
The next headland served Woodrow as Summer White House,
from a silk chair dispersing Haiti's parliament at gunpoint.
Thomas Jefferson Coolidge's brick with portico,
its dance floor mirroring sconce candles, his first memory
fire at their Bowdoin Street House, men dragging the pumper.
No plumbing, only candles. Fanny Longfellow's dress kindled
from sealing wax fanned by the sea breeze,
Longfellow stifled it with a rug as she ran to him too late.
Caput mortuum, a smelter, but not for sins of the tribe.

30

Procedure in that bony furnace is single,
party membership no coolant, no offloads feasible.
The pin-striped chair loaned to Woodrow lends no sweetener,
Madisonian presbyter at Kettle's Cove
baptizing masscult propaganda before the Duce,
smothering Randolph Bourne, anointing Lippmann—
the trampling and roar of a bewildered herd—
Madison primly, Lenin hysterically. Bomb plots,
so they posted cavalry around him on his ride to the Capitol
to declare war, Chief Justice White, formerly
9th Louisiana Irregulars, inciting cheers for the professor
with his rebel yell. Pin stripes, and as at Pompeii
stones trailing where the walls were
through grass combing sea wind.
No delaying your decapitation: truckle
to the preparers, promise them your calc ashtray.
If only variety sucks up variety, then only twist
smoothly tightens twist, only curvature rounds off destiny.
Girl went, and girl, rescue vanishing, patient Hammond
teasing his gizmos past static, interference a moiré screen
of the sensed unspoken. And of Ike's appalled thumbprint
on the strategic scheme for obliteration
to this day unrevoked. Haul oil to my burning lamps
among magnifying mirrors aimed through lenses
out over rocks and surf.
Silvery under wave run, flux-threading whammo-fish,
pinging three times toward wriggly sutures
down the cranium's rivers. An engineer at the Towers
found molten steel dripping from the cranes three weeks later
and came to his own conclusions.

31

And in February when air flows arctic, warmer water
rifts into plumes of sea smoke,
sweetly thermal physics for the skull's art.
Stand back from Rafe's Chasm, Norman's Woe, Kettle's Reef,
and when the bus transmission drops out
and conductor Shell Mayo shrugs,
take a two-horse cabriolet to where the Aborn burned.
Our mothers have been saddled with much madness
in a shut house, wars a slow cauldron, and they reached out
to their son's wicks, lighting them without knowing.
Time for the cattle run to be cleared, where no one
broke fence past the assassins to rush the bunkers of gain,
they were still there, but we did not go after them anymore.
All for a heap of scrap and fine wiring,
for a lasered heat sensor guiding payload now
as for a naval gun then
cammed to a tilting platform at 25 knots or strapped to a scope,
the whole sleek thing tucked below waterline.
Damnatio yet absolution, their knot unswirling in tide wash,
a choking birth caul to split with tempest and to spread with peace.
Cryptanalysis did not set Minister Gulls
on the drabbled hotel statues.
Sousa did not run through a set of his own marches
because the Chief Justice sat there among parasoled ladies.
First-chair trumpet outdid himself not simply because
Sousa's left hand punched the air in the second string
of *The Thunderer.* Contemplation is digestion
nakedly in full daylight, paunching out belly feathers.
The moon's titrated decommissioning per diem is the earth's job
in each bone cooker, repeatedly and without comment.

32

The cast for *The Cradle Will Rock*, locked out in '37,
trailed Welles and Blitzstein twenty blocks
to The Venice, taking seats in the audience section
with Blitzstein ready to do all the roles at the piano.
I tell myself that my solos answer to overtones
and therefore go in brave company, not as meat
bleating in the stalls. Yet to go in the numerous
thus walking, an acoustic chamber of one,
is to go twice-herded. Sounds wrong-side out,
yet so I've been had. So I cross into day and carry it.
The brave infant of Youngstown did not flee back into entrails
when Ray Gun gutted the basis.
Womb, wame, wamme, gamb and gambrel,
horse hooked high and war man dangled, belly's bulge
and a leg up in the gamble, dance your smack-down
werra the fog of collision, sturdy boy. Even the finch
tucks up into night leafage through branching complicity,
flinging from feeders into high oaks with Charles Ives.
When Blitzstein dared begin, Olive Stanton stood up
and did her opening number, and no one moved,
and the rest of the cast rose one by one, belting it.
The moon's rerun is the sun's sidelong resurrection,
and the night that set me onstage with two aides
in slings over boiling water, a gussied cow swaying with us,
allotted only one stroke with broadsword
which if I missed would drop us. *Thwackdown*: her spine buttery,
the uncoiling gut splashing,
and between dousings of the house lights
we gulleyed over the cauldron three times, contemplating it,
inhaling steam, the house silent with us.

33

Doris Hatch is not made a durable soul
by virtue of being remembered here—the ideology
of Western verse to the contrary
notwithstanding. Standing in the long rain, truly soaked—
let that be confessed at the heart of the line.
The emperor arsenicked Mozart
(*The Requiem is for* m e).
Sokrates standing for days, and Moses in legend
running while standing still,
or standards ventilated by grapeshot, rippling stationary
over a forward rank,
all of this doth bloody philology grace
via the crotch of Venus smelling of hay and sea bass
slotted into furrows by Pequot farmers
for their tall corn. But the ecstatic
emergence from her: that stance rises through every office
and statute, the fermentation of ferment is peace,
and we trail blizzard custom warm, sealed
in constants of tribal solstice.
These subsist—but not the precious *Thou*
substantiated by the *I* in its long song.
Olive Stanton, too, who could start it over
even after it was ousted, *stant*, *stare* and *oust*
all outcries from a root
dangling into substrates of breath—she a Victory stopped
in her take-off from a Greek prow
at Samothrace on a landing in the Louvre:
yes, she rises. And my refugee waif by the tracks
stands with her. As long as we stand up with them.
Out on their trek to The Venice, with Stone of Lightning.

34

Through carbonized mist he brings her,
Herakles after pinning death
with two falls to spare, freeing
Alkestis veiled in toile—
rumpled deathware translucently
spun to lifewear, she maintains silence:
in red-fleck crystals, pyroclast
throughout dust samples
from Towers 1 & 2, from Building 7,
microgeodes of iron beading her veil,
buckshot hurled in the billions
by thermite, and sidefall pleats welded
much as cheddar, boiled then iced, blisters milk
through furnace into evidence, reeking
of sulfur its midwife, with sulfur's transform thermate,
the welder's butter knife
through I-beams: these the wardrobe
not of rescue but reclamation, vulcanism
scorching loss so as to sear denial, quick hurt
then long release. With bluefire torch and glared visor
she must fall through 40,000
tons of steel members able to resist
five times their load, then return in such dress
not in six and a half seconds
but the length of unwavering pledges however shabbily
laid aside—come back to honor, accuracy,
the temerity of fact.
My own employer later, who had managed cleaning teams
in Building 7's hotel,
her muteness: this grit stole wraps her as well.

35

You are already underwater, Athens—Plato's
Atlantis: Sicily's quarries, the Caspian
pipeline for Azeri oil,
also the Trans-Caucasus gas pipeline,
all for a high temple on its outcrop—
where dolphins nudge ring-bubbles through each other,
blue plex lines drifting the friezes.
Davie, thirty-five years on from Murmansk,
realized that when
most aware of who I was, and what I was doing,
he moved through Graham Greene's Vienna,
his generation revenants, the Ferris wheel still turning
above tanks *left to rust in the snow.* Bonaparte
stretched his line to Moscow, into autumn,
not from some Russian lure, or his own bent,
but the whole mass of choices,
rippled facets heaving:
Tolstoy returns to his dear singulars, sucks in breath,
the day dazes with clarity,
he has her peer into the nursery
where the kids are riding to Moscow
and invite Mama to join them.
On the shelf an unsleeping hussar
of lead and paint
rides on through lights-out, in brass-button anabasis
holding all that potency
in the two worlds shining through each other—
gantries and smoked-glass towers
and one raft half-sunk in a pond face, while overhead
wave-crinkles, a swirl of shoal herring.

36

At the Ursuline Convent in Quebec City
granite soaks up the sprinkle of high night,
low hedges halt the wanderer.
The bronze abbess and her girls don't hold me here,
yet this check deepens, a glue
vaporous in corridors, readings, shoes
at anchor near iron cots
rippled by the under-river of days.
Anonymity is what you do
beyond the conflict. And beyond the great,
as here where the lords of two empires made out like bandits.
Then Roosevelt and Churchill sparking cigars
from one match. Order gathers everything at one moment
to itself though itself is what it gores,
and the fight is black, and there are no breathers,
and fog is the drift of the wolf.
So, as here, can I meet it, a feminine
fate, the sequestered fame-
less praying of the stream onward and down
the knees' channels, into reddening foam?
The hallways in there gleam under smooth vaultings.
Still teachers: their hardness crimps and soothes,
either there is no wilting
in their stem or it is pure miniature.
The Second Division Band in bearskins, scarlet cockades
and tunics, stepped out like toys
with the same animus, fearless, the same black shoes.
Whatever nails me here breathes
shy of analogies, no sure
beat or rule drives it, cadence of boots or beads.

37

And no phantasm of some former life
grips me. Victor Hugo
stopped in the ruin of his old school staring,
the leaf-strewn courtyard of the Feuillantines.
Which is it, man or imago,
And what lives? I am convinced by these scenes
as by the thud of the carotid, yet their bearing
pushes in on strife
bedded in Paleolithic velvet, antlers fuzzing while pronging
the first walls of mind. A hunter's
Balanchine footfall makes prelude, while these sisters
teach from a stranger wound,
not chased and hemmed in, into which
any other wound might crowd to glove itself. Red focus
of home human godly demonic.
They become the bleeding they need until quarry
stands there. On the edge, now,
of never again such stillness.
Signature acts wait porous to that seepage and grieve
the open that once was
while bearing it inside themselves:
a repopulated hunt within a depopulated fate.
Many the gripscapes pained and pinned onward, but single
the thrash of max poverty. Wasters
not, wanters not,
freelancing out along the edge
of any clue whatsoever, they breast cold mist
with men in the dawn chorus,
reverberating
to bunched droplets in their gather and hang.

38

Ruskin worked the guilds, Ruskin chamfered the edges
on Pound's toboggan, Ruskin the delicate
bolstered men in the crafts and at lathes, taking his students—
Wilde, Toynbee—out on road-building details.
And waded, while eddies swirled behind
those balcony-high sterns lettered in gold
Emerson, Dickens, Wilde. Therefore posted himself
at the unselfconscious oak podium, salting
a goad's footers in gratis nobility:
Rome's dawn starch, Gothic Greek, alpine steeplings,
duty to good winning no profit and fronting
the mist machines of a not-yet new age
with moral process worn on no sleeve or memo
unspoken though unlost.
John Brashear had children tour his coal-shed shop,
my Grandfather among them, to inspect
his lenses, telescopes, burners, tools—which have led, via syllogism,
to L-3 Communications slash Lockheed Martin slash
PARAMAX. That, too, is procession.
Parti pris des choses—taking sides with things—
now there was a step. Just when, however, will creditor-gamblers
pay up alongside debtors when *things* go wrong?
Or be the first to do so? On that improbable foundation
rest the blood-flecked poetics of Dante,
seven centuries. I walk barefoot into
quickfires of desiring, a fleeing stag
as fugitive slave, cervus and servus, my runaway
boiling in my own bones: obedience
exhumed and numbered by L-3's tracking sensors
trembling to distill liquor from blue ash.

39

One can fantasize the single blow
under which sandstone layers would meld
and the great orb tack otherwise,
shoulders back, numbered jersey rippling.
The conductor's opening baton lifts to rock ledges
where it floats: an outlook over tufted valleys
quilts aeons of labor down there,
my eye from the flank of Monadnock is in that stick,
the entire string section holding at port arms
peers at the maestro for release into action,
the furrow-browed tympanist crouching over his depth charge—
outbreaking sound compresses
laus et vituperatio, Buddhist Barnum alternatives
I reached for in otherwise plain teaching—
which good fortune made mine in a backwater
from a plain deal desk in the brick schoolhouse
facing the Erie mainline through Cambridge Springs,
canning factory percolating beside it
through recess. That scene still drapes scrim
behind instruction that has mattered, whether
from Ian Watt's sleeved hankie trailing
River Kwai malaria, or Bruce Franklin's harpoon
piercing his Melville lectures, or Platonist Jon Ketchum's
magnum of *Faculty Killer* for tenured guests at table
maturing in his off-campus lair, Palo Alto.
Not corked there, though, *azure cælum*—the ooze
from flesh feeling the skull but sailing as
onion-skin air-mail envelope, fire-resistant
imperturbable extract
of lifetimes, body of the longest river.

40

Ready to pitch C. G. Jung in Pittsburgh,
the amphitheater growing populous,
I had ten minutes to go. Down-corridor, a classroom,
the black desk stopping me—
when he taught math there to undergrads,
Father's red forelock broke in a wave that he swiped
upward to the rhythm, maybe, of Euler's theorem.
Then, my turn: from Jung's red-bound book, a painting
thrown behind me on two motorized megascreens,
the metabolizing individuum,
as if a Navajo sand phantasm in billboard scale
from a cell's twenty microns whose core, a star-point fort,
sizzles with saw-tooth voltage.
Or sluiced: the same lines write the water glyph in the tomb texts.
All the primes known as *Jung* were in place by 1912,
but their co-primes, blooming from Euler's formula,
exploded from him during the slide toward First Marne.
He learned: one must stop inside the crackling expansion,
hold fast to the image, make it speak, bulk it out.
Emerging from Basel's terminal, Father saw
E U L E R on the entablature: *One tough theorem,*
all but saluting. Those waves of voltage
I could not decode for my crowd as vaulting co-primes,
but I alleged—the proof caked in muck—
that they broke Jung into unforeseen scalars
under mass slaughter and the rock pick of guilt.
Alleged, minus the corollaries:
that the Bomb that Father sheathed inserted
the push of never stopping, crashing
out through the end-wall of the fifth act,

41

one impulse from an infernal *would.*
That encryptions, well-tended by this theorem,
blast release but veil the consequences.
That the Big Heat, air's lift-off glyph, fiercest scalar
ever to push outward, is pushing now.
What thrust at the alienist each night detonated
in slow-motion solitude: five years in the writing,
sixteen in all with the paintings.
How delicately paced, the countermeasures taken
against implacables. The bastard City of God
hangs inverted in her rain-slick squares
through the globe's rolling blackout, turps streaking ice.
Next day, alone in seminar rooms framed and painted to honor
the Poles, Czechs, Hungarians, and Romanians
who stoked the mills,
I choose one, lock the door behind me,
fold open a hand-carved oak blackboard cabinet,
floral vines chiseled across panels
by a cabinetmaker from the old country,
and stroke three words partnered in my sleep,
staying with those co-primes, not churning out art
but stopping with Samuel's *He got us this far*:
    Thane—warrior in service, and a child at play.
    Wolf—wulf, lupus, virkas—pack warrior who also plays.
    Who suckled the twins and rends *wel.*
    Deer—Tier, deor, dius, cervus—the twelve-point Christ tiptoe on jet.
    Quarry of both thane and wolf: the goal.
    Not *truth lying somewhere between*
    but scut lifted, nostrils flared.
And there my chalk breaks.

42

Yes, two boys took titty between hairy flanks,
dragging on wild sustenance
then dinner from Lord Woodpecker.
And chalk-trickled slate streaks Tiber
but also now every spring
gurgling under the hoof's cleaver,
Pege, Hippokrene, thimble tributaries of Connecticut
tucking sky into earth, drawing competitors
in shifts to guzzle at dusk.
Look long into these, and the empires wink out: if only
repeats did not spell discontinuity—
and rapids crash unbroken beside fish-ladders,
both waters past possessing: the impounded
riding the unowned, as Chen Changfen
saw it from his photo airplane,
the Great Wall heaved by a limber spine
and crumbled by sobbing Meng Jiangnu,
her man dead on the work gangs.
For past managing it breaks out
across tundra, strings of caribou flank-kissing
in pass-pass over cloud-deep water threads
between wolf harriers—
boreal duns and tarnishes
undrying in spring melt, that aggrieved shamaness
throbbing them out of perishing into generation
where flat in a scope on a copter
a loper pitches headlong through puddles, fraying knot:
the twang of polarities
in dying worlds as in a living one, most living in dying,
antler prong scraping lichen, sedge, bluet.

43

Andrew Mellon's Institute engorged
Carnegie Tech as Carnegie Mellon.
Hoover's Treasury Secretary was brother to Bollingen's underwriter,
but I have not gone back there to spit out the seeds.
The fabled hollow with power plant
cooled dens for panthers. The museum's grand staircase
frescoes the locos Grandfather drove,
his multiplier of coal into the firebox
pluming as pillar of cloud by day,
tucking under as it swells.
With three-coupled engines he snakes in
sixty-two Ionic monoliths for every face of the Institute,
pressing the springs nearly flat
as he looks back on the curves.
A square crib for Gargantua three stories sunk in earth
to hold the thing low-profile,
a Parthenon for turbines and neurons.
Knuckled couplers jolt chinking from parade halt,
china dropped in the pantry, Nabokov startling awake
en route to Coker College and Spelman
to their domino yank down the line.
Carnegie Museum's head from '26 to '46, Andrey Avinoff,
the Czar's man, then diplomat for the Whites,
swept up that top spot from his position in Butterflies,
with pal Nabokov coveting the *Lesser Purple Emperor*:
twi-colored at tilted wing fold, native to Russia,
blue house in the mind.
These are not illustrations to an unspoken thesis
but riders on exponentials
crossing a three-barred equal sign at Mach speed

44

to float, talk's accelerating buzz
cresting into talk's blessèd cease: Verlaine to Celan,
from the condition of music to the condition of muteness—
yes, do go on hearing things, but listen for the surplus
in surcease. Even with munitions falling:
violence too is a prayer, an imprecation, demand gone off the rails.
A German tourist on the Horseshoe Curve, Grandad's run:
Yah, zer vuss a plot, to blow it oop und shtopp sings a vile.
The teacher in that red book is a gardener lecturing Krishna-like
to the dead, back not from the trenches but Jerusalem—seekers
of conscious baptism or wide-awake dying burnt at the stake, Anabaptists
still hungry, yanking the doctor's doorbell, rattling the china.
For two days Jung heard him scooping
from the hoppers of cosmology, showing them how
to put the hoe into themselves, and the clamor ceased,
and the maid resumed folding air-dried sheets.
They arrived in unmarked coaches. And always will.
A gardener: *nourishing himself from himself*
to meet famishment in the horde, our dead dearest yet unfed by us,
grease to our evils, and mist through pre-dawn rain
past cripples and the blind warming their backs at daybreak
along Kirk's bake house wall, London's East End—
a Second Marne in the '30s
(the *Oxford Junior Dictionary* 80 years on dumps *fern, ivy, buttercup*)—
while Avinoff and Nabokov, their nets lacing sunlight,
are rolled over like hoppers toy-like in the mill yard
and then set down empty:
anthracite under pinned wings the harvest,
for the dead seek it too,
blue cælum, bitumen's crinoline heart.

45

Gaining a ledge, the trail
leveled out through stucco huts with stone chapel,
the Churfirsten, everyone gone to vineyards—the years, the years
under the scarp, from its brow in noon silence
an arching cataract
stipulating headwaters of the Ganges
where no such could be—of course, yet to deny that twist
in the neck of incinerated morning
will not do. Past the last roof
my years slowed to these boot soles in grit
and a boy crouching where a shelf one hand wide
zigged across a rock face, and pitoned cable. Far down
lake sand paled into cobalt.
Squinting at the miniledge, he sprinted it,
me picking my way—then forest, switchbacks for hours,
and I found him hunkering over coals, ash drift,
down-lake one flukey star burrowing as far in
as it stayed far out to enter,
the drenched one sifting ash, this age a bulge of mercury
blue now gray-black.
                                        Aevum novum
would not be our mundanely lethal hiddenness
Code names are for assets, not targets—
for a star thus sunken shimmies with time a-comin'
through a lake's wrinkles
                                        and the epoch Shiva's,
terminus trembling with breakout:
no man's to have alone yet coming to one, to another,
sunken, soaring anabasis
and in their twin points one fire, ævum
inextinguishable yet also unbegun: novum.

46

A sax player, shorter than the others,
stands head down after cradling
his alto horn, pale metal
not quite as old as he is—
the beachfront restaurant is younger—
between trumpet and string bass
keyboard and brushing drummer back of him,
his left arm crosses to grasp the right
dangling, but no, it hangs stiff,
fist resolute. Violet dress shirt,
face occluded, he is his own churinga
nestling inside that fist waiting
to be secreted—
his own hidden body
which granddad placed in his palm, stone or oak gnarl,
advising him that it was himself:
Bury him, you will be safe there,
talk to him, he is no one else's
while the clasping arm crooks tight,
a hook on the stone axeheads
in Latvian passage graves,
each an owl goddess, arms across her breast
eye-beads lasering death, even prone there
her posture erect, to greet Iraq's teenager Inanna—
and when he does lift those headlamps
it won't yet be Paul's resurrection body
corpus subtilis
its withheld riff cascading
but the whole form of some totem
reaching to grab worn brass clabbered in medals.

47

A loop stitch pulled tight pinches the gather:
thus Prince Andrei bereft raising his son,
the white tunic in mothballs, Andrei having it out with Pierre
on the ferry, mental arm-wrestling
having it out genially while out at pasture,
uniform resignation, uniform at hang,
on a clear day the same arc as over Austerlitz
but only then that deep draw toward cumulus adrift
past Bonaparte his idol
looking down at him with an adjutant: *A noble death*—
the demigod ordinary, small in the saddle
achingly sky and sky the figure now
pasteboard.... Thus the student of power relations
at hang, superior gaze across any gathering in any room
to any purpose on earth at hang in the loose gather
mounding unbuttoned, each gilded nobbin
no longer even laughable, carp in the pond
less than serious, his manumitted serfs occupying
a liberty no longer serious because no longer palpable
to him their liberator, capacity
itself unserious, incapacity emptying
into that blood muck under cloud sway
neither laughable nor serious but an absorbent
hinterland to the continuing scene: scrim
at hang behind his pinch-lipped wife
gone to her death shrieking in giving birth
and the standard he grabbed when he charged, the rake he inspects
with his factor, the drag of *still seeing through things*
after having it out congenially, a separate peace
the dry hell twist gnarling a barren oak.

48

Then to the Rostovs, that crake tree gathered
into their park past the turn: their youngest daughter
from the night window above his own ledge
gathering her substance tight to itself squeezing,
bubbling at smudgy summer
moon foliage, her breath timing
the take in him still on the gather, and as she rustled
back inside prattling, the old oak broke new leaves
and, without cause, that stitch lying untugged,
the sky at Austerlitz soared again over the dead, the great man
again eulogizing him then dwindling,
that vault and its drift
and his wife's dead face, his friend leaning
over the ferry railing, and that girl, all convened
in a certainty:
                it was not finished,
everyone now must come to know what he knew—
for living was not a property, he could not
consign himself to it by freeing his charges, because
this fountaining past his resurrection
into hell beside a carp pond was, and it was not only
for himself, and could not yet become
fully itself if the others were to go on
apart from all this, they had to gather and hold it
as a mirror does, live it out with him
all in one sky. All skies in one abyss
blueing cirrus over
the sun's bed—a seal's frolic shimmy
down his famished dive into turquoise compressions
pulls the gaze past its own salt and guilt
into, not the named, not their ground, but this.

49

The continuity of knowing what is the case
down to the sump in the cellar, up to the ridgepole,
sideways to the winds—that tensile thread
from Spider Woman in the first-nation tales
will still serve with neuroscience now
for telling us what are the mind's fire, and instinct,
and their leaping yoke. Continuous
pull on your tackle and fly, brown silver glister,
neither beginning nor end
to your whispering slice of it, let there be
as many such good mornings
as pillared Delphi brought the ambassadors
from the shield towns up-valley
to its treasury, amphitheater, and sulfur-reeking
carney narthex through olives.
What I can hazard is that such unbroken awareness
issues from a fight. And that
the brawl is both secret and outright, the opponents
far in yet far out, and that their bond
through struggle, if fed and weathered, pulses
into expansion—
broader through the stream's
brightness but also its draw from blot bottom,
ramped luminosity with power-black suck.
And that Americans bring it hunger from the genes—
discontinuous from Eden and thus driven
to gather back in Fuller's way the old transplants
that broke up in her wreck off Long Island.
Thus too *unhandselled every hour*, the wild
Concord option: go big, glare with pitch, rawly.

50

For the fight is not sporting. Greek hip tosses
were for bones broken, shoulders dislocated,
and correspondingly
the festivities around victory
shot for the colonnades of sunrise—
brutal though we may be, we are still fastidious
about what the odes tripped out
with dance steps portable into battle,
stork steps under fanning shields backed by skirling
pipers with no kilts. The point was to win—
grabbing after a fire that seared retinas
swart with effulgence, a sinterizing same
against same, opposition
all the keener for that—a fathering masher
launching the stretch limo of mortality
into zero gravity, orgasmic worm splendor.
A rumble sustained inside attraction itself
hard against the boundary, alchemists
calculating a discus throw from the salvator mundi
to a savior working the power reaches of atoms,
bronze plowing earth, Adam's grunting exhale into
reunion. John Paul Vann
barreled his pistol jeep down Vietnam's back roads
believing he could map the void zones
in his bosses' outlook, Emerson wired
the circuit breakers past overload, cartography
and mystic welds their double-column bookkeeping
for enlarging a shared darkness
through jumped-up light.
A scorching track warms each bare runner's blear shadow.

51

The seepage of engineered torment
upward as improvisation
and downward as bleeds past an averted gaze—
getting it done on the spot, over against
consigning it to trolls
while maintaining an even gait across the bridge:
that osmosis both ways
in one membrane wide as the globe
nowhere fixed by coordinates:
such is the flow
sunset-wide across shingle
pipette-thin through morale,
slurring its words to itself
because shy of phrasing
for the joints and nerves it feels and wields,
staying nameless while serving
the abyss one is, its force nowhere else convened
and nowhere so furtive.
As if one were to say: it is here, now, present
and personal, where person ground fine
seeps away; imperium.
The price! The press: unsought payment for service
in advance and unwilling, shoved into hand
then the hand wrenched. No one wants to be around
when that happens, Jacob's avoidance of the goat
trickles him straight into
goatish encounter with a Sumo wrestler
who pins him on the beach at first light,
shunned horsepower nailing him as mitzvah.
A horse's kick, our forefather—
a sound man leaves that open:

52 / *quantum*

the electrical engineer
realized later that the thirty-two transformers
at substations on service levels in Towers 1 & 2,
no fluid in them, unburnable,
were so massive that they would have
plummeted well before the floors might have pancaked,
rocketing huge holes going down.
But he was not about to voice the inference,
leaving that to his interlocutor:
before the collapse, visible explosions
on the lower floors made unnecessary
any of that heavyweight
penetration by logic into the softer
materials of the supporting premise. No trace
of the pits they would have plowed,
and no trace of them.
The elected stuffs in these situations, no matter
how exquisite or brutal, leave their hinge holes
after the dismantling. Augustine's Alypius,
resisting, was hauled to the multiplex and shut his eyes
but at the roar
looked up and like the felled fighter
was cut through. And grew avid. But at last remembered.
Engineers like doctors
ascribe what shows up for them
not to character but to points framing a curve
which they cradle—forgetting nothing
of the long crowd they have seen and heard, the fear smell
and amnesia—but they stay, cupping them, symptomata
those things that fall together.

52a / *wave*

[Yet more than engineering:
lateral puffs down the sides of both structures
unstitch fabric but also the sky behind it:
only by staying with the illegible event
does one illuminate it
with more than aviation fuel—
one force takes aim while another perks in the belly,
here in world-bellows,
eventually: the advent from adventures.
And solids turn sketchy: *shapes alter their materials…*
change, and then change again—
Dante's smoke-rolled schemers are and are not
Peter Scott's impresarios of *piggybacking*.
Dare to read those puffs
reading it out: perforations rip down
along twin seams leaving tall gaps,
blank prescriptions
from evil for evil unto evil.
More like a weather system than a structure (Scott)
beneath which pixelflicker and buzzfuzz promise safety
in wastes of waylessness.
Not as Nicholas von Flüe
dropped his weapon when the weird singer
decanted honey onto guilt and sorrow; neither our man
nor our mess, yet only a hive-deep berserker
sweetens the wild.
What further armor to undo, little boy twiddling
leather thongs on that breastplate
toppled near Aphrodite's nightie? Ares wants
to knock off work for a while.]

53

Sketching the limestone Saint John on Patmos, New York,
through jabbing glints from the sea into old age,
the Burgundian carver has me keeping him young,
here lying out in the unrelieved spasm
of totality. Politics is a brothel,
a fiddling learning is seeping, while this herald stabs
at parchment, a slab of it dangling down,
an Afro lifting his plain skullcap—
shading a laser gaze, this mocks times
and the curl of times, the history of hell
blurring heaven's gate, the left knee tilted under
as the foot's arch encaves tender shadow.
Mahler studied this man—
silence halts the finale several times.
What you have fought for does not survive so much
as pushes past itself, envelope
of the day popping, a boy
chasing and reaching his chromed bubble. It is the world
before Monteverdi but after torn Dionysos
lay revived in a bath. I catch the churning
above his page, those paws blurring
a polar bear's in their power stroke as seals fade
with ice to sky melt, not three miles but sixty,
clownish hips barrel-rolling
as the cameraman strives to keep pace. But already he catches
those wheeling mitts coiling furred yarn
from a bobbin in that other twilight technology,
no hunt but a gather, filamental, womanly,
already in the too-late aperture onto encompassing
weaves of the whole, threading out of sight.

54

Exodus, the treadway out of impasse
led by Coroner of Aromas, shepherd Honoré Masse—
Gustaf Sobin has him shatter the crock in a votive pillar
and inhale *une odeur suave*, someone's dust—
perhaps Saint Genès, or Dardanus who portaged him there
after narrowly failing to save Rome by marrying Galla to a Goth.
The shepherd in Sobin as Osiris breathing on Horus: *You and I are one.*
Not Orpheus calls back the dead, but their own flowing spark
toward that fluttering gash in the aft of the *Hindenburg*—
the Anabaptist martyrs as roving static
igniting Jung at his villa, primed for them by dreams
foreshadowing war's outbreak: his work hence an act of conscience—
thus, no patents on the dead: complicit, we keep the line open
fire-dry through wet smother.
Dawn Romanesque the sanded upland of some unforeseen
maximum: thus
if I say nothing of what matters most because
mostly I cannot, then
only the assault ridge eroding the heart bastion
paves the road outward.
A bouquet brews oozy stems and aromas
but not respectability's long game against conscience:
no one has that kind of time, certainly not
a man whose life has been
given back to him. Alkestis came back because she too had elected
to pass under the eraser. The road hence
rounds implausibly to crack the walls not fallen—
bulldozer exodus as homewending, on lilac as on the mind waking—
and to shoulder Asteracea, tough Ice Ballet, her spear curls
offering up while shielding the prong host.

55

Gone missing is grief,
still unperformed any giving-over
of privileges not won but taken as due, blithely
from posterity in tatters, ribs to the wind—
look straight into the world
and hell's broadswords Himalayas tumble
yet that very seeing enacts
God's thoughts God's thoughts deus sive natura:
they will be in what we are in for, the as-yet unmet
layers and lourdes in those thoughts, magma injections
the Reed Sea a jellyfish swarm not parting,
red sky at noon all year.
Gone any tongue for sifted
lamentation, glottal sashes flung wide
in pled remission: gone for a nice wind-bowling flat
as rigged lightning field, guy-wired prongs
drawing down charge by lifting
others to meet it, breakaway
upsurge into downthrust, blæw runouts
through chartreuse—
                                        crackling this time
into no blue teardrops
from the glassworks at Sainte-Marthe, earth-borne
to a scuffling boot there, pallor of late sky
surfacing through clayey dust,
therewith the first motion
they have known since shattering
past the blower's grip on his pipe
bulbing a parison
from its blow mold: luminously workable, the mass
of tinted grief prepared to distend, burst.

56

From tomb stench to the wanton chaste fragrance
of the rose, only the reddening moon punches your ticket,
Saturn behind now, sword melting to stamen,
eclipse as a double devouring, flaring torn linen—
thus fold them not, rumpled bedsheets spread the harmonic
all the way in from cold ringmaster
to the endogas generator of daylight,
debtors to fate being granted brief holiday,
gene drag or star weight to the contrary notwithstanding—
morale no longer claustral to corridors
through the malls and down the black basis—
witness the signposts passing:
demon Mars and demon Venus a-swirl
in the consommé of poultry and lean will
as the full scorch diameter swings over
and the circuit rewinds, ice-rings flinging buckshot—
decay wafting even from a babe's breath,
mortuary lees bottoming innocence
to anoint the beginning in the end,
for the open-pit mines of the micron are bleachered with fuel
and a renouncing not a signature style pours caulk
to swathe the crack-born seed:
yet none the less, and ever, one strong secret breath
would recreate the world—
and so not only some free-jewel expatriate distills
crime reports and eulogies from nicked bone, stained post holes,
but a kid-king in mufti
does a Fool's handspring, landing loony-eyed, squat,
his spook-sport interregnum whispering
to our burning scene: him too shall we disparage?

57

Like the cold mirror
hazed with a half-fuzz of mist,
pointy array on a pineapple or grenade
which gave, when I streaked it with my fist, arcs
of face and shirt, mine—
farmhouse sagging among
sapling-studded pasture and kneecapped barn,
oblique pastoral pinging its held note:
like that, the taut mute alert
for eighteen months after I came back to this country
which drifted scarves of raw sensing
around me toward fathomless killing
anywhere, at any time—
rub at the smudges on that slab fog
and it gives back glimpses of oneself
beneath unappeased red,
miasma abroad and at home,
old, fresh, about to be,
wrapping your gaze though you swipe.
Athenians on the morning they poured the new wine,
their streets the previous night
echoing with dead Raritans and Sioux,
sat apart and mute in their cups,
each an Orestes:
go down with Nurse Bubbly
into shared foundations,
the court inquest also,
rack slaves for their testimony, it is all one
and so the air gives it back
if you haven't breathed it for an age, a life of times.

58

As the empress of Hades her serene mouth sealed across
stuffs of saying, their generative gels,
laces breath with amnesia,
so the seam unguents from Crow's head
elected before the stem wound the spring
darken like light in bearing.
Cloud seeders ack-acking cloud
with pouches of silver iodide do not listen
for sandhill cranes,
as our heavy-metal bands are past listening
for their father Baudelaire or Thom Gunn their friend.
Yet Homeric armor, both hard and yielding, cladding
the soft bodies of rangy young men, and old men,
already was a city-wide scrap heap
suddenly upended, pouring for hours. Though not
my métier, these are still my meat: the Waverley novels stretch
their chord progressions
over yokel migrations to new Shanghai and China's Pittsburgh—
for the old order, mine with it, burrows into a last
spasm toward inconceivable rebirth.
Gettysburg's Joshua Chamberlain
refused to go on teaching Rhetoric, draping
his study with battle flags,
thus gauzing his tunneling hip wound July or December,
not to go back but to feel forward under fire—
for sidelong drip the mercuries of spring rains: our Satanism
secretly ministers to the destitute
by dinning the vacant lots out of sight, past hearing,
and the bone-littered caves inside hearing
below the ledge at Chauvet.

59

Blood murked from homecoming through the veins
distills blue from purple, purpura regia
to the rhythm of sidestepping, even a crown
being won along curved routes, blood waltzing, arrows falling:
a flawed initiation, that will stand,
rather than the complete kit with spare parts.
The full job takes you out, *It is a terrible thing*
to fall into the hands of   blood's springpoint
recocking itself. The former marine captain J. A. G.
John Schuchardt and Carrie with warwaifs and Camphill
retards in a roomy colonial Manse
This, maybe, injects a small homeopathic titration
and brick star in the barn floor—one Bosnian's gratitude—
with Walden's hut replica uphill, another's thank-you—
amending Miłosz to Merton: *The novel about your country*
in this century ought to be set at Gethsemane—
never again Zoffany's *The Sharp Family*
on their three-tiered music barge *Apollo*,
royal surgeon William at apex
lifting a tricorn, his brothers archdeacon and abolitionist
among satins blue, wheat-gold, and slate on the women
at fortepiano and lute, brother James cradling coils
of serpent tuba: their midday Water Scheem at Fulham.
For no: from the Agawam hill back of this Manse
Massachusetts blue clears through storm wrack
as it does behind the painter's grandstanding Sharps, but this time
over a stone circle trued on star points,
John's boulders mounding
through late autumn grasses, pacing the gaps
of effort ever finite: *Let us love, let us fear.*

60

Hoop Pole, Roast Meat Hill, Skunk Misery, Jail Hill, L'hommedieu
these road signs through bungalow woods float
episode, epigram, the jumbled deeps
of which we are capable and the veils, too,
drawn over them. And this for only one
compact among the peoples:
beneath it along a low spine split watersheds
east to Quinnehtukqut, west to Quinnipiac,
Ponsett Ridge to Cockaponsett then Mattabassett
rumoring the effaced.
France alone clung to administration under the occupier,
bundling its own children
off by decree, the intent being to secure France's future.
Whereas solidarity canceling analysis means Rosa Luxemburg
choosing, though she foresaw the ambush, to join
those already in motion. Speak with someone, anyone, long enough,
and feel the withdrawing wave take sand with it
not in depletion only
but also the finite clasping the unbounded,
thus the name on a path: no story.
Students of extreme survival, inviting narratives
from returnees, catalog persistent
tale elementals—stream, structure, whole—
and most tenaciously
the unscripted advent, unanticipated
in the drastic or the bare playout,
of a hand offered, the risk pusher
who found a chink and pulled the tale teller
on through, salvific bung-holer far on
propelling the mouth: brother, sister.

61

The bills of lading show it:
measurements for plate glass, Venetian,
sent to the London palace of Elizabeth Regina,
plate mirror, all of it, specifications
suiting what the builders in her time
were requested to fit up: a snug octagonal
chamber with one door,
all we have of it now the dimensions,
hand bills matching the hefty depth
to those eight walls, floor, ceiling.
What we are sleuthing shows it back to our inquiries,
sole place where she could strip herself
to see what they held, all of it,
as such: not for mere errors, but how it sagged
and wrinkled, sprouted and discolored,
yet still carried, enough of it, her rex intelligence
eight sided, vertical,
unfoolable to the eight coigns of an unstable realm,
to tavern cubbies, or the lark palace
in summer trees, in gullies of wind
still as hair down a creekbed neck, to herself
visible in angled aspects, all of it.
So they come on the run to tell us: Amelia Earhart's boot heel
and femur break island surface when Mozart's skull
ruptures its Potter's Field, teeth matching
the scanty record. Navigation there, too, proved chancy,
a gross fracture scoring the parietal
en route home from beer and gaming
and improvisation with crossed hands while being held
upside down, and yet

62

Through the Logos I mocked everything that exists
and myself suffered no mockery, I leaped in the dance.
Yeshua Amadeus, corpus of light in a cave:
offended, we backing off,
seeing that it can be broken, the seamless
Nidhana chain of suffering, a ring meant to be broken,
yet backing off.
                    Enter into
nothing less than the whole with your all, and say, Glory.
Dried blood on the atoll and in the mass grave issues
summonses to the round-dance—
and this crux severs all perishings from the condensed world—
gaze into the electrum, a mind that completes what you are
and which you know not.
With five senses, that makes six mirrors
showing both known ground
and the slap I gave to a dear woman—my unseeing deprivation
rebuking a helpless deprivation rather than carrying it,
sorrow having wheels, a cry's axletree
whereas cruelty is its own assizes.
And so, sit long enough to outwait delusion: my sole place
is set for me, six- or eight-sided
by ambush as:
        cemetery by the sea, Old Saybrook—
from day's crosscut edge, completion
once the stroke stills
and the slab teeth regiment space. A completion
still percolating past the causeway
and half-moon headstones, their trade
between wolfish outposts gargling
the congregated bones—yet these are not what I hear,
it is their thrust into life,
everyone present, none virginal; all in all.

63

For moaningly their ledgers bagged the wind while disgorging
Maori flutes, whiskered puppets, where now kevlar jibs
lean in to scour the channel—
none of that lashes me to the landing
where they throng now, my unmet dead
well-fed yet starved, loyal yet betrayed, stalking the blood ditch
for a jolt of memory. The causeway dangles
Vietnamese anglers over muck-dredging swans,
their brats cawing through mesh fencing—no ragpicker
to scan depths on the trash surface, no bowsman
to read embryo storms from wave lace,
for here, Finisterre:
miles out the puffs tilt caelum
over sourceling giveways of ground. And I might have known
that already I'd met my hungry horde
when self-hobbled I scrabbled
far toward an exit, where they must have coalesced
because it only seemed to be final—
yet their need and not my appointment
sets fire to the ordinary
and cobbles sky onto shock newness
now massing in the swell
that creams the walls in my hands
as it whelmed past Thuravalluvar,
poet in stone on the spit at Kannyakumari,
slurrying shacks and fishing boats, men asleep under them,
past four hundred pilgrims perched on rock
where Vivekenanda's shrine
faces outward. Those were spared. Seeing hearing
shuddering at being.

64

The wretched: bowling unseen through ball-peen,
building froth, spinning sand and scuddle
to withdraw no longer as one thing,
And you think we came out of nowhere?
Where at last we are, what was can be no longer.
Horse hairs cast by a bantam queen
into a demon's fire
and it came, commanding her to kill it,
the whinnying, saving factor,
and to splay his shins to the four quarters
and tent with her babes under his ribs,
the barney skull to one side:
no sooner had his kerosene exploded
than the call: slay the very power in you
that booms out from basis,
pointing the way by withdrawing:
slash, vanish into it, and conquer.
Fetlock and glaze-eye in the muck,
that was Turkestan. Play it, Sam.
A panicky filly, finally shot, bookends
this medicine at zero
only because two war horses frame its calm amplitude,
the abused pair who foretold his death to Achilles.
Play it because *Les Misérables* foams across the big screen
as buds furred the canals
in box-hedge medieval lovers' gardens,
uisce-washes of color
shielding no one gathered here: whole peoples their faces lit
as soggy ice floes cartwheeling down the berm
of a March-maddened river.

65

Photographs: take the square
format of Robert Adams's *denver*
prints: take the overbearing
all-dissolving, everything-hardening
flame from overhead:
take it and bear it—
the submissive do not, the yearning do, bearing it—
away on all sides equally
in mute hardihood, hardly to be endured
unless you take also all that exists and prevails
both as implacable, unplacatable, unplaceable,
positionless even unto
the impositional,
fixed unto the very fix you are in
(the poisson meet poison in these waters,
the most rending
rendering the most healing),
the sun in the eye of the sun bleaching *I*
so that no-touch torture
may proceed medicinally:
goggles, gloves, earmuffs in that cubicle
inducing bonding—
the long aporias of trail-breaking
benefit the tourists of a day
but the god of the diggers is a newborn glinting the seam:
stand there in the 24-hour stress position
of Sokrates, the week-long posting
of Pachomius, spiking the golden-section ratio
of the irrational solid.

66

My moaning dozing tabby is no adjunct
to Hekate. The potentials past
her slumber scan my next move
toward which, though awake, I crawl on radar
toward the line, sheet metal
shaken backstage,
howitzers blending out
into the falls on Oahu
where gobies, their mouths French-kissing
water-curtained rock,
spurt upstream ledge to ledge, blind couloirs
and failing strength winnowing them:
our clicketing coach arrowed fields, windbreaks,
artillery pacing us,
and her sleeveless blue dress,
freckled hills lifting its low yoke,
were both reunion and mission—orders
unspoken, unquestioned: go, converge
on the capital, locate the new house,
sleeks lipping themselves up the last stone
through the brim comb, on into brief spreads
of river, wave into trough
among sedges, their mighty
yet veiled appointment—
though once that portal framed us she had vanished.
Gatepost herms there, ballistic red clay, neither
weapon nor god but still standing into
advent drumming in, how not take them
as the forceps, not for what she bore
but for those agonies dearest to her?

67

Victory the momentary god
ruptures through from the coals,
hieratic because yesterday is in it,
lathered because sweat and olive oil
roll down its limbs from strigils
in slow surfs of grit, elaifa
with helios, scented leis across hell,
mortality in it because
those scrapers are carved in ridges on the tombs—
tomorrow in it because
it shoots itself through drastic flash,
ignition rolling out of itself, a morning
wink improbable from murk—
and beginnings, shining from the egg
pitilessly to everything except
what pulls them forth, bypass the act
to spill aura. Delicately, then!
Mark Catesby's eye in Marcus Aurelius' wiring
would set bison under a rose acacia
to scrub their huge Afros along its trunk
calming, browsing, the will to run things
in the great man sacrificed to that friction,
a North Carolina tree still there because
it does not surrender to powers
that would rub out the whole, it still prinks
perches for Monarchs:
wing scales a world roof
zigging a mountain-range graph of eroded
unerring reach, flagrantly
homing through their scarped scraped voyage.

68

Lodge the éloges in futurity
out of shame for the present,
hive hopelessness in star emerald
to meet the dung fires
of rancor from the generations,
and wind, and whirlwind,
treasure the croup-toned honkings
from angles of geese
on schedule into their dwindling north,
oak moss on the march.
Prod the rituals
but no makeshifts, mere
sorrow a mush laid
steaming in dayfire.
Da Vinci's eyes could track a bird's wing
at frames per second
sufficient to get us into flight,
could trace water beads from a fountain
pearling down poured arcs—
but at what table, and which our meal
this side of breakout
and rampage? Once and future temple,
to we hoarders of lack
slo-mo our strobe mind to your proportions,
hold us to them through
the long unbuilding, to all that they
have made evident of the unmade,
rise through us again only if
pillar and cella
and teeth under the eaves find us ready.

69

And in Wolfram already
rode an up-to-date battlefield medic,
one E.-R. surgeon has stumbled on it:
a chancy chest wound, and the knight's
lady helpless, Gawan stripped the bark
from a branch, rolled it into a tube,
das bluot ist sînes herzen last,
See, it's the blood pressing on his heart,
and she sucked it out,
and paleness flushed, blinked, chattered,
and I forgot my coffee.
The surgeon leaned forward, his speech
wholly accountable to fact, unwrapping
fresh ancestry for his own skills,
but also a point rider sallied out
on picquet, and I saw Parzival
at halt staring down at blood on snow
remembering Blanchefleur—our
down-at-heel destiny: through the bread-warm café
its chill measured us,
a search for blood's vagrant cup
and the hunt brought to a stand
close by, their mounts pooting, streaming,
for it was not the hog's trace
halting that briar-decked host somewhere near us
but an inventory
in each extreme face
of the wound blessings and their powers,
for these harried their own kind,
the realm broken.

70

Thought the plow spills curls gleaming then crumbling,
a mold shines onto its casting lifting away,
a seizure focus seared
from the lobe's trench
hovers for days then re-seats itself.
Plato's table in the mind
waxes the oak under my elbows,
Mark's Chapter-One baptism shreds the skies,
schizogomenou, and dunks *you* in the plural,
with Jordan meant to pour from everyone's shoulders
to a forty-day exodus among jackals
and schizzy nimbus messengers.
The groundsmen of Greenland melt have their ice sheet
grinding on shelved nerve
before it voids into brine, as Berkman
ripped cobblestones from the brain pan
before upending the street.
The next turnover
therefore invites me to walk upright
while preparing to drag me.
Piling on, pushing out, the day crackles
from its shrink wrap and fool's cap,
abandoning Lear to his maunderings
as it exits into night.
Even so the foot said to the hand:
Let us come to an understanding.
I am your stranded assets,
your unburned reserves of angelism.
And when things move, that is because already
I am the ground that consents to move with you.

71

Full moon through 4 a.m. quilted cloud
does not hang but sails—or it does not sail
but swings into occlusion to spin back,
self-valving lens orbiting unchecked crime
veiled volent, spade-headed fealty
of the serpent tunneling our spine,
a pearl cold-cocking fire. We will get there
on time, but I did not say such,
her companionship the breakwater
rendering that an impertinence,
our full corrida afloat in her aware smile
through intermittent rounds crumbling
the perimeter. Already
fulfilled: whatever time is, it draws
devotion down its condensary, schedules
tilting the vortex of a nude decimal.
Hand did not need to seek hand, their mating
memorious in the whole body seen,
a steady-giddy lunge of sprung tons
cradling us over that plain—
or else the betrayed ground pulled back under our warmth
passive no longer, withdrawing
as an arrow shank when the bowman
spring-cocks his carbon arc,
little Greek pulleys and gears cranking,
and rallantando lowers to aim. Thus
into me she flew:
the Big Heat and die-offs, baled miseries—
her face exists not to dispel them but front
this turn, moon-sun amor pouring to steel.

Four

THE BEWITCHED GROOM

bucking insanity, surviving guilt

1

Inizia—
withholdings, curses, all their damnable protest
under my breath seeking some absconder
Hell! bits of smooth glass in the shatterfield
of the beach splayed wide by ebb,
choice marzipan spat out by process,
gleaming in your allowing
ease: no further, no deeper need I burrow
to find your donation.
                                        All resistance slides
in runnels out to the shine, placid seepings
of release.
            Zero disc in the wind rolling
hints of itself, the key ring at your girdle
hourly undoing prisoners' bindings
and ting-tings through the running lights of a freighter
in the bay's roadstead, miles out into a patience
assured of the wharf's hug and unloading.
                                                                    Never
late the meeting—punctual even down
the corridor of crime, as the ripe pear confides,
as the shower flouncing from cloud swag announces,
On time:
            my hand is the work of millennia
and thus too its work, yet in thanks becomes only what,
lifting and valving into the unmeasured,
I give you, rebeginner of grasps and pourings.

You visited? You abandoned? You are always here.

2

Specular winter oaks ripple sundown scrim
in the world-theater, spectacular
fencing to barely possible reflections which,
should they rise,
bring up ultraviolet
lights in the audience, before anyone
can adjust. Even those who fling on
their dark glasses peer open-mouthed. Stet,
keep the venerable script there! No bleedout,
we did not pay for that.
Preceptors and manciples, the benches
for rowers with chains, oak blocks hammered
in thrashing rhythms: where are they, we are
beyond that. We do not pay with that.
Saw it towed toward us across the Lagoon,
a squared-off tower old style but welded to a barge,
eight sides on the cupola,
gangway, then galleries stacked as at La Scala,
Rossi's way of saying that it comes and goes,
it pushes off, they park it. How is it around me
if it pulls away, growing smaller?
Santa Maria della Salute,
sun sparkle floating her, she too as if
the model for it, hangs one thumb wide.

3

Speculum as a silvered round flipping up,
the sprung lid on a powder compact
from a purse circa 1940. Feminine measures
preparing a face silky as the cutwater
on a liner, doubled in its wave curl,
blessèd force completion. Spectacle
the very bath of the tribe daycrack to shuteye,
filmic digital glaze circumfending
against exception and perception by way of interception,
Capability Jane off-limits,
no nine-day medicine hop Night Chant or Mountain Chant
sweating on painted sand under the smoke hole
after which, says the subject, one actually
feels like going on clean of the whole business
fresh crown to toe.
The mounting galleries, if one completes
their loops, pile toruses to the clerestory.
And they say, the sentinels, that a vast doughnut shape
defines the remainder of resilience.
Seepage, glut, fistulae burst the world envelope,
fire glint where all and none smash the berms
on the path. The antecedents, having piled
into rock ledges, have not stepped aside
yet we do not climb down them, measuring their backs.

4

From *Ho, beau!* to *Ho, bo[y]!* runs the guesswork
(*Your vittles are good—so we've chalked your front steps*),
canned beans and carrots from Mother, even so—
our windowed back porch their mezzanine:
Plato's menu *oaks and stones* likewise
dispensed with luxuries, empire, and war Q. E. D.
and three years post-Nagasaki
that migrant working class was not yet unwelcome,
midpoint on the Erie mainline and steam still a contender,
thus our water tank and coal tipple near the school,
the jump point slow out of town.
Yard bulls in the '30s had pointed men to the trains.
A certain shock derives from coupling
plot type with purpose with political leaning with major trope
then running the combinations: historical romance not just *talk religion and get food*, but pound ladings LOAD LMT
though Tocqueville dusted off in a town of two thousand?
An emigré led me to him.
The cinder bulls in Plato patrolled for emotive phantasms,
bullets peppering the gondolas:
he wanted those young rulers to theorize it, that is, see it all at once
like watching the games at Olympia—
a fully loaded freight winding through the mountains
with several hundred people on the tops and the sides of the cars.

5

I had retraced my route on a wet day
still missing the address, a slow horse
on a fast track at dismissible odds, and settled
into the mood brewed it seemed by the very
fog forming, late p.m.,
and vacantly locked onto a chocolatey smear
of earth tenanted by yellow
bulldozers and front loaders. Another
commercial engorgement along the strip—
and there it mounded, the spill.
The crew was somewhere on break, my own gaze
still a sliding thing
until it snagged on that heap
warmer than the dank drift and thus slanting
three vapor plumes
intact through murk: Erdsprache,
Erdgeist, l'esprit du terrain:
in any language, utterance
for its own sake at its own tempo, regardless
though disregarded. Not
submitting, yet shaping. Morning
about to explode there,
cotton rifting unwounded blue—
Constable at cruise speed hanging out the window.

6

A sprouting surge relapses less often
than it advances, whereas backsliding
blackmelts down fuzzy pockets.
Shall Jack Hawkaway draw his lath cutlass
against a Stealth wingspan? Hooker and Clarendon
I failed to plumb on my syllabus
when Hobbes hobbled Washington, though Jeffers had elided
species impudence with coastal fog, and Merton
withdrew in order to advance. Dutch Republic or Roman,
oak and stone fell stranded in ironies
from the Silenus-faced man—thus will my troth be
with onward Trewth, smudge-folded in sway skirt
and prickled braid, long-wall mining
having spavined her flanks.
Thus Jack Hawkaway shall draw. For Rabbi Akiva
lifted with booster tanks from his stone seat
through rainbow-twist galleries of climb
before the flaying combs, and Alexandrian Christians
stacked glass on glass in rivermind, their faces
pressing between strata
to corners of the same garden,
mica-bright though mired, exchanging
exigencies of territory and rule
for agonies of the mirror.

7

Slim James Hansen in floppy outback hat
before a megascreen
plays a Viking twang lamenting his decades
of spot-on ineffectiveness—
confession that sifts dry rot down ancestral timbers—
not simply this Dutch or that Irish spray of seed
tendrilling forward with mash destiny,
for the argument and the bundled lines buzz here.
Four hundred thousand Hiroshimas each day
the heat surplus he tallies
not from the neutron furnace overhead
but our fermentation vats.
Tony Luhan, alias Mountain Lake, Mabel Dodge's fourth husband
(Frieda and D. H. Lawrence in his back seat)
observed, half himself and half renegade, that the sun
for the Pueblo required their help every day
crossing the sky. Meaning was not at issue for them.
Them: Tony Luhan was Mountain Lake, but Mountain Lake was?
A question lifted once, idly dropped.
The sun lifts, apparently.
At the mesa rim guests leave the car, wipe their brows,
swiping the forehead's bindu, Shiva's wellspring
bunged fizzy, a gusher
to guzzlers but to the wise the fount of days.

8

More than greatness, in the great there explodes
from strata at point origin
dislodgement by spasm
inscrutable to them, life-death's blip caesura
until their grasp around the lesion reassembles
what no one until that seizure held fast.
Leader, who drops the plummet, colonel at column's head—
these merely suggest the demonstration, monstrum,
a monstrance they hailed in T. E. Lawrence, who walked away, shunning it
because in such castaway taking-hold it releases
others to themselves.
Schismatics, sectarians, cracked visionaries, Balkan,
bleary voters for Armageddon, oppression's tatters,
off-throw from revolution's aftermath, spew of Vulcan
smearing the imperial forge: Jews and Greeks
for Spartacus, driven from Rome with Margaret Fuller,
sprung prisoners, Hungarians, Poles, Decembrists, zeks.
To set out on a path is also to guess its end,
to link in loyalty is also to take in the harrow's
iron tip where the gash unzippers. To understand
is also to wish for pig ignorance
yet hold both in a blaze cup
and bring them closer, drink.
They enter here stunned, yet as authors, fulfilled

9

in following the draw of cyclones,
systems beading into
lowering cells, cumuli walling off
most of the sky so as to gleam one plot
of earth as fated. Those people would say
that they simply stood, or bolted, having been pulled here,
having duly followed. Surely
they are drawn, they erupt, yet break into
a glared treasury of innovations, their own.
The psychotic head earthed by Perseus at Corinth
and fused to Athene's breastplate,
haunting Victorian fantasy—that dread
has not stopped them, nor the cold retreat
from its muck tangles. A probe shaled in mimicry,
bouldered in scree from heaped witnesses,
entombed has pointed the way. Thus rupture's
ozone freshness does not lag but sheens
the dunes muffling blind surf.
By ejecting from the main drag
Peter's crowd meant to sidestep history,
yet they gawked where the weld fizzes, the digger's red tunic
budding over the hole. I am to meet
mitzvah only in injustice and destitution,
their pierced gazes.

10

Mr. Biesty does cutaway drawings for young and old,
having a large box of leftover parts with which he hopes to build
an aircraft carrier. Mr. B. lives in England
bequeathing us TANK: Raymond Williams drove one,
but not the Soviet T-34 blueprinted
in my birth year, ground broken for the Pentagon,
a hospital some day, thought the president,
once and future medicine. This thing
had no equal in the world which it entered
with its shrieking problematic gearbox. Crews trained
for seventy-two hours, and then the Spring-Point
for the sun's crawl advances one degree in seventy-two years,
sheer racket in there. Wedged fuel and ammo their pyre
twenty-one-pound petards slung by hand.
Malraux's crew in his novel. Then the movies.
But refugees—Trojans, not yet Romans—built otherwise,
their mortar scooped from grief, their jamboree on landing
a funeral dance. Whereas sentiment strokes a silky steel
through the innards of philology, as through jungles
when a sleuth engineer zingers an ace's *Hellcat*, his clue
a worming Japanese tracer, concertina sans teeth.
Dear heart how like you this?
Sungu ok slungu   snuthga steini
sang they and slung the spinning stone.

11

Self-reliant, self-malignant,
straight up through the buoyancy
of life-death, stream-side sycamores unravel
the wiring bared in a house
under demolition. Or raw March vigor
veins the day with pole scrimshaw
incompletely etched, eczema
streaky then spotty in Morse Code:
a ballerina jatte in great age
frozen in the camera obscura
of astonishment.
Yet all this is lived through, lives itself through
whether I am prepared—
as each rollover unfolds
without previews and is not welcomed
with smile rates per contact hour
but becomes evident: a flash, mind effectual at distance,
as past praise or opinion it cups
the mountain lake tremulant at dawn.
Or as fate, not baggage-tagged,
is to be read slowly.
For still living into my lowest, where dirt
crumbles like aging cheddar, and support
claws for news: that shaming grabs me.

12

Even Boston's North Shore meets the south shore
sold to us for our silence.
A barker strode here, morning a reamed clam shell,
acrobats and tents having vacated.
What I wanted I still want, freight spasming
with climbers down from some peak, masks off, tremors
pinching their mouths as they unbend by inches,
until a gull slaps my shoulder, popping the sense that I unbuckled
from my load long since.
Low-slung cars at a crawl, drums fuzzily
jolting smoked glass,
half-soothe my blood—rhino heart, elephant heart
as if throbbing here
past their murders, galaxies still flaring
having gone black,
so I am working the last turn of bronze,
unbuilding, taking as charge a tousled looby
whom no one sees,
hot for zanies and flummery, as if spreading for him
past the beryl truck bodies,
and the band's muffled tinkles & enameled glides,
god grass as bedding:
rhino heart, hippo heart and the whales, home of the tales
and my best doom.

13

Into that boy drained the barker
mute at last? It has got to be less occluded
than such a shuffle, merest funnel trick
unless malady calls forth its remedy—
yet that is just what it does do. And so
on back toward *A*, by undoing
not with tamping wing
but goat foot or horse hoof,
with horny dint through accumulations
so that conditions drum into
their first inklings, so that the least aim will carry
the conditions of that aim:
no restoration of all things to the last grain
but the first kernel struck,
Pege or Hippokrene,
with the gash force of all it will gush. Feel
our way back along the line's punch, fail not
(tank commander Bion)
to scan the Canal du Nord at Bellenglise,
pools lining out
behind a four-horse team scalloping muck
upslope with an artillery limber
past the sagged girders of a span
down at Antietam, Agincourt, Armageddon.

14

Late '70s as Cinquecento:
heaved high by young men, four turtles
capped the pocket square, their elephant
bronze tails making for the fountain's jet
day through night in cobbled walled peace:
Jewish Ghetto and the Rione Sant' Angelo's
palace cluster for the clan that roped in
all that coolth for themselves: names, water—
January posters announcing Arafat,
Hanoi on the rebound, El Salvador
soon to taste the lash from our proxies—that gurgle,
with bubble-float sailing the divinatory pool,
might become, it seemed, great counter-Rome
among the peoples, the elsewhere of a pause
unforeseeable and pacific,
a rank herd and their shepherd
rivering a boulder I had stood on, Via Appia,
their muzzles tucking leathery lip across
the eras, present in packed bleating,
the man hailing my gnosis with raised hand.
Thus, Piazza Mattei. And a downstream age
aborted now. Red-lined. When linkage
is still scored by spotters beyond the runways
as did Chalmers Johnson in the '40s:

15

type, make, and serial number as in his day,
but now the code on the tails shifting,
Gulfs Streams and Lear Jets
to Syria, Egypt, and Uzbekistan
where their headman boils the take: from Kennedy, Raleigh, O'Hare
the bill of lading *e x i t* so that los desaparacidos
do not lift from the stadium in Santiago
or in Cherokees through San Salvador
but from home—in cold suck, tumbleshoot
filigrees from fixed ailerons, micro-ice
down the eyes of chugging swans
as down my shadow here in these lines:
plump dolphins still captive to those four youths,
their cocks at ease, they tap over-shoulder
those turtles into the basin,
urgent squirmers: for still, theirs is the one
masculine solution that has not been tried. And so bubbles
across a dark diafane wink off, blue into terracotta
rippling on that mirror at ancient
noon when the dead walk and children chase
raucously there, with a young pair stopping
to drink each other, bearing witness
no less old though unseeing to the blank
mutualities of all these powers.

16

Between twin frondy towers
Lady Arachne has spread shining trap lines
and tucks her sleek buttocks
at their picture-window heart.
My shears cutting in, she shinnies a bright path
crumpling through her grip,
a feminine Jim Thorpe
tight with collapsing means,
backfield coaching, Oklahoma juice
poured out, her scurry
not for quarry but draining height
recouped in shade, leafage of the deep floor.
As if Babe Zaharias, née Didriksen, the Sieglinde of my teens,
were dropped among the Steelers
in summer practice, our village gridiron
in fact cushioning their yells and topples,
pibroch or the Great Music
in river-valley slews of Gaelic ceol mor,
shrill skirls from mills in Wierton, Wheeling:
Johnny Unitas, Joe Namath, Mike Ditka,
Aliquippa, Beaver Falls, Aliquippa—
the country it was and the game it engendered, its coup
counted by Winslow Homer's twin bass leaping
for the downfield bomb.

17

Lead ingots were marshaled in leaning pods
like hoplites where the fight gets thick and nasty—
yet that foundry spaded raw pellets
with devout pours to the forms, slowing me
to its river as the foreman went for the gate
and stamped, snow stitching his pipe's cloud,
and donned a putty felt hat.
Rippled sheds now swim the train window
with his vanishing, a moment's monument,
the flash of his mauled hand deflecting
toward justice, searing inquiry
leaping categories and their forge
as if it might total every score.
The nailers went with him, by money's power
to inveigle froth from its innards
and suck the air from pine sweeps, hen coop, creek pasture,
and the humped gleams in rat traps: by two of eight
lithe arms from a mother dome leathery
bulbous blackly scudding, their suckers
soundless. The felt cap rumpling that head
retrieves one detail from the long mind—
twin felt caps on the Gemini Dante scanned,
marking them out for king-births
down the chewed corridor of change:

18

twins which their own suns plucked into alignment
spotted from his fast train, their ferment
of foreordained freedom, predetermined release—from
long night, the good hand—this must and will
be, yet will aim its doubleness singly.
Thus, naive no longer: neither dare I untangle
the close weaves of love and anger, their rolled wool,
hair and sweat pounded flat, nor simply echo
such soundings. Nor turn from tears. All burn
between the mauled and the good hand.
That wolf yell pulling back from the cab,
jolting lunge down the slot, failing nothing of mine
though it go helpless,
these extract me from the dead hours,
for I ride a pummeling loosed, a ramming freed
without stint, to ask: might they, then, be
mesh mates, death and justice? As swabbed oil on metal.
Skulls with entrails, moldings carpentered
through stacked halls of the palace of the eye of the mind,
or that chapel cornice of skulls, the Grisons,
blending to whitewash: these pin pitons for a ropeless
scarp's fine name blown from the ear, climbers
ant-like fading out. Justice just there,
as oil sheathes the sliding of steel, soundless.

19

A red Genoa rug
must have been what I saw and would rub day-long:
the weave rolling up its underside,
its entwined reek of hay, disposes
loam footers through sifted litter,
that exhumed spread the very mesh in the trays,
the teams off to lunch, buttery wire
graphing loop stitches grown from fate's grid.
Over the whole stretch it becomes clear
that my thoughts have not been mine, ever.
Passion stays tabled for fight, sleep, need,
burgundy once blood hives oxygen,
the themes of leadership and the curves
of mind probing matter's engines
condense to specks trembling past the wharves
on the rim of the pattern, the deed.
Feeling grew like the brown shin shuttle
pushing from a dig, crude, essential.
And a man giving thanks blessed my head
while I slept. On waking I recalled
his act, his reason, and my being
as interlinked freedoms, the unrepealed
laws of the heretofore, and the young
weave underfoot as one thrust, one goad.

20

A boy returns from an expedition and regales his parents.
Lights-out, he puts his ear to their bedroom wall.
Taken for dead, Er, Man of All the Peoples
comes to on the pyre, the battle's damp cord wood,
and climbs down to rasp out his embassy,
and the reviewers quibble over details, those made superfluous
by the histories. Look for him on the docks,
ballasting his disgust in the tavernas.
Jan Karski, the Polish Errol Flynn
smuggled through a tunnel into the ghetto,
surfaces in the chambers of Mr. Justice Frankfurter,
and the eminence says, *Do you know I am a Jew?*
Karski points to the pyres, lays out the numbers. Silence.
The exile Polish Ambassador motions to him:
Don't say anything.
—Frankfurter turned his back to us, three, maybe four minutes.
Then, looking me straight in the face: —Mr. Karski,
a man like me, talking to a man like you, must be frank.
So I say, I am unable to believe you.
—But Felix! You cannot say this to him, as if he is lying.
He has been checked and rechecked. This is his fourth mission.
—Mister Ambassador, I did not say that this young man is lying.
I said that I am unable to believe him.
There is a difference.

21

I know better than to call haulage
of the heaviest, the unchosen
that chooses me out, by a light name,
for transitus of the bull or the tree rules—
yet motion that we share we give name and time.
As if the century were
an express at night, lamps on
blankly in the corridors,
and looking out into blurred passage one saw
the dark unmarked, and then, slumped
at car's end, the attendant
nodding to the abrupt sway:
there the spell thins, we are of not only
what hurtles us, for mere breathing
can draw in and lift
out over the rain-streaked roof
to let all shoot loud restful and terrible
untouched by the space it reams leaving
nothing even of
its own ramming force: neither
The Franz Schubert nor *The Phoebe Snow*, keeping
neither wet steel nor the smell
of oil, it threads to hum
and ozone in the great peace.

22

Neither a bad moon rising nor a slipped disc
in the cosmic spine, but the mandated
mandala of gain and loss, smooth, round, and
Never tired, said the Tathagata
and *Unceasing*, stipulated Yeshua.
And in both was it the same concrete activity?
The committed realm stays at hand, yet when spoken scatters.
Hardpan road and a crushed coil
of garter stopped me, much as Dogen's Inmo sermon
had hung for decades among my generation.
In Japan, a mere remnant: here an alluring haze.
In that sermon Seppo was being implored
by his platoon of trainees
to spout the saving formulation,
their sleeves a churn of inquiries
when Gensa broke: *Put the question, Master!*
And he swung: *What if it comes along,*
the clear mirror, what will it be inside time?
And Gensa yelled, *Blasted to smithereens!*
And they watched it tinkle to shards.
Whereas we watched a binding allegory of reflection,
Hawthorne's compact and Melville's crew,
go under the tank tread and rise as de Man's seminar.

23

With this tale Dogen wanted those near him
in the blast with cork-bobbing moon
to be no wider than they were, exactly
that span of sleeves and hems.
Mirror, concrete external of the extant.
The compact excludes slavery: that much
we seem to have secured, though even that purchase
can still be lost.
The Japanese came from their silent rubble
to be masters of audition:
Listen! to halt us on the road
to hear the tar, and the gravel, and the builders.
As Sibelius walked his baffled composition students
through a meadow
to hear its overtone series.
As bucolics hum the moleculars of epic,
or as Ponge's meadow,
where he buries himself as his name,
Préparé pour nous
par la nature, Pré, paré, pré, près prêt,
hums the field of the world,
or as the stance of the Senator's daughter
at her window, unaproned, bone-tired,
held her the makeweight to mountains,
Miss Emily.

24

But unheroic, the next step:
siphoning the large into the small, resetting scale
while declining to lend measure to anything
that refuses to look its counterpart in the eye
and so look itself in the eye.
What remembers me is my words
before they were mine.
With stick tip I flipped those strands of gold braid and gut
from road to meadow, for once letting the sound
go unpursued.
Potent draught, mead, med, honey wine
socked in mindhive, haymow barleymow
so cut them down minne and menos
love with force,
deify neither, and through their weave, mnesis
the saying, menen, at the back wall vaporizes:
menses moon's round on itself
as meadow nests in mederi, listen,
remederi medicine that plows
the mead down through itself.
The great Finn knew he would not be believed
yet only in that way gain a hearing, into which
the ropey arc of the corpse sails briefly
free from its cotillion of flies.

25

How you are singing:
from that you show me what you'll be singing
in durance hale or vile.
How you survey a groom flat on his back,
eyes shut, the mare peering back around
and a crone gawking through a half-door with torch—
the engraving by Hans Grien—
hold that for a moment and I'll tell you
what you'll be saying about the stylishly
cloaked injustice working inside sunlight
on promenades jollied out
past your front yard. What you make of it,
the straw-and-dung-flecked scene,
whether or not you scroll witchcraft into it
or construe the mare as a stud or momentarily
affiliate the stall boy's jacket, its pleats
and ripply tucks, with high station: though these cogs
in the gearing of your take
tooth a definite sequence, coloring
and culling a specific harvest—these tell
less in the mound weight on the pan balance
than how the macro already in you cups it,
the man you are, the woman you are, leaning
in at the stall, breathing, not breathing.

26

See: their warrens are laid
mansard on gambrel, hipped roof on mansard,
mosaic metastasis of inquests in a hived
mosque of vigilance, the vigors
of twelve elves and seventeen giants, the eld of all watchers
unsleeping over the sleeping
breast and crotch shadow of the continent.
Eighty billions, one hundred billions for reviving
the Völuspá. For fixing on the Quaker graveyard in Flushing,
its low stones grown-over, the many
nameless there: picking out the hipped roof of that Meeting,
half-pyramid of granite where George Fox orated
and John Bowne resolved to declare himself truant to all authority
in his *Remonstrance*, sparking fires
still smoldering in the unkindled.
Let it indeed be resolved: that because the universes
worm each other, integrity stands forfeit to tunnelings,
so that what might save stays closest
yet unmanifest, and even the fatal encounter
will be one more moment.
Nerve, nerve and edge!—ira et studium—
in their prospects now there remains nothing laureled.
The noble act inhales singularity
and exhales homeland, banking on trust
as the hawk banks on mortal thermals.

27

Philip Kintner, eighteen,
Comm Technician 5th Class, 102nd Recon Mechanized Cavalry,
in the rear of a jeep through post-surrender Munich
could see in every direction almost everything
save the tops of this and that pile
and stood up, and discovered that he was
the tallest thing around.
Professor K. led his students
through the Peasant Wars, Luther's backwash
and Melanchthon's apologetics. And perching on ladders
he caulked high windows in the Memmingen archives
and drew forth Judith, Yuditt
who murdered her child, *die Frau sehr schön*, condemned
to drown in the Iller in a dunking chair
but lifted by all the big men in every direction
to wear chains, their number and thickness
decreased by further intercessions—
and with these minims from the fathers
the vast Christ inch winched them past their iron ledge:
imperial pardon coming after thirteen years, links
caked with mud making the forge mutter
across cobbles all the same,
this he saw across the ruins,
das Schöne.

28

Who maketh a fair showing
where none looks, who keepeth counsel with
herself, for herself, to no one
vouchsafing that which is not safe save in herself
islanded, tide ripple rolling moon glaze
in where no hand travels nor eye gropes.
Mute sister, this one finest lost thing and
thus the missing index
to the flambeau crone, her brand poking
into the stable, swart Hexe,
exiled creatrix, stew fixer, bone with filth:
that one gets the publicity.
Whereas the other, not because you are yet worthy
but simply out of
unavoidable conjunction meets you
in close, half-light
setting a drink pearl-cool there neither pre-mixed
nor menu-ready, which if you drink
in clarity you will step past the Hexer
by a hair's width into savannahs. To the low
stream with carp, *m e r e o l e m a*, their gleams
not quite touching, dorsals not quite breaking surface,
their gold streaked with red:
I am worth your tears.

29

Trap and trace
the trap and trace order,
the production of any tangible things
may make an application for an order, magistracy
shall enter an ex parte order
shall not disclose that it is issued for purposes
by inserting 'routing, addressing' after 'dialing'
not specifically named in the order
by installing and using its own pen register
on trap and trace device on a packet-switched data network
which is to say, the Sir & St. Thomas More kit,
namely, proof upon one's own body
touches no one because it holds everyone
by inserting 'or other facility' after 'telephone line,' ex lex patriae.
Read with the mind of unborn lightning
    and thread the day like a snake.
The hand hath 83 bones, nearly half of these
the palmars and flexors, followed hard upon by 18
extensors, all serving 13 bony phalanges
(an unpledged double fan of them: not Franco's)
and one week of days called the interosseals
serviced by three linear pulleys
which dial back to check the bowstring effect
(should Agincourt fail me, then may my right hand…).

30

Bill Spanos has returned
not quite alone to tell us, but returned.
Greaseball the Southern sergeant tagged him in boot camp.
Schnecke, slug, from a civilian foreman
in the work camp near Dresden
after the firebombing. Names come and go
(his brawl began at *The Bulge*),
the one that sticks being *Kinddttt* and less than kind,
from the foreman when Spanos finally steals food,
and from a Czech-German matron in bed: *Child—*
who echoes Hardy's Fates after returning
(*Speke, Parott*) or gratefully
opens to the percussion in East Coker, trepidation
that would plant the timeless shakes onward
Keeping time, keeping the rhythm in their dancing…
Feet rising and falling, Eating and drinking. Dung and death.
Onward simply to catch up.
I was inter esse, I would now put it—
there is no self-blame in *Drive all blames into one*
but a body blow says: *Here, this is it, it's yours now*
cracks beneath bootsole, heel, that is where it gets
interesting. Under the dancers
below—in the midst—ignorant stunned stableboy
down there in the nowhole under the fire.

31

Guardians without grit topple alive in the grave. . . .
—And what did he aim at, the writer?
—At trust worth keeping, flame in the untrembling gaze,
embers raked into his rib cage.
Feathery hammer under my breastbone forging images...
—And what did he sound like, the writer?
—Wind through larches, after-beats through drum heart, bells
over lakes: wakes and weddings.
—Those sounds are his. What say you?
A Stone Pheasant striding through a high meadow
seeking her young to shield them, freezes:
magnify her twentyfold, give her the ape's heart, and you have
rescue as both white fire and choking smoke—
the Cheyenne warrior sang, *Heyaheahoyeheyehea*
I am coming through the big smoke
line of peaks at last visible
And fishing boats came from the northeast to Dunkirk,
blunt high bows
Aniewoon here fray the Brocchh! scraping
keel in the shallows
of course taking on board all comers, many sorties
among the shells
and here or there a nick in the taffrail, every sixtieth
fray the Broch:

32

to grant no greater reality than is due
to the greater harms, nor to
redemptions: to sit them as would a goat shepherdess.
Bowls of the fountain, each flows and rests
—Why did he stare into splashings, calling them peaks?
— Displacements settled him. Running as repose.
A minimum—always inadequate—of humanity into situations that
should not exist
(Antiphony of one, come in, we read you, we read you:)
—all ways of humanity into that minimum
        —*equate that* please
—ways into humanity
        —*adequate that, exist adequate to that*
—a minimum—always inadequate—humane in situ, situs, site
        —*inadequate*
—the ways in find the site—abrupt, singular in its minimum
        —*should not*
—existing past the site
        —*n o t*
—at a minimum incomparable and therefore standing forth
        —*always not adequate*
—past equilibrium it stands into gusts of situation
        no, n o t
—the incomparably minimum siting its stand
        s h o u l d n o t e x i s t   —does

Guardians…rests: 'Stille Leuchten,' Conrad Ferdinand Meyer; *A minimum… that should not exist*: Thierry Germond, the International Red Cross, 1996.

33

Nature skips no steps, *die Natur keine Sprungen machen—*
count them, take them in series, but with two feet—
inculcate in yourself the fact that waywardness
governs walking, as gene master François Jacob
tallied his own errantries, not the coastline's
seamless meander but an incalculable progression
taken without voting it in
(no ballot of white pebbles, no lime chimes to calc with).
Inculcate the recalcitrance of the totals:
force it through your head with your heel—
not that the wild step kicks back, but it toys with you
(he lay in two casts at the Val de Grace hospital
deliriously investing the rippled ceiling oblong
with his desert war and the Paris he could not stroll)
until you accede and take it (from doctoring to biology
and hired for no discernible reason by Tréfouel then Lwoff:
warmly, "We've just learned how to induce the prophage"—
blankly, "That's exactly what I'd like to work on")
thence in ten years to gene expression, the operon,
the off-on kickdown-then-kickstart in microlife
seen eyes-shut in a cinema cavern then phrased to his wife—
Night science the path from *Gaullegothique* wounds to splicing
the lab's recalcitrant research programs: a kicking fate,
toys, kickshaws, quelque chose. Qualis causa.

34

Rapt exegete of rocks, heron-legged
strider through Mongolia, Gobi,
pick-axe and canteen timing the incalculable
with the forged and the poured
since the too-muchness passing
through the mass that one is
wants the compass's thin iron quivering down the aeons
of our restlessness.
Angular Teilhard ready
to peer into anything of worth,
show me the recipe,
paint the cliffs at Chou-kou-tien
into squares, flapping graph paper screening
the open secret:
here yet lay embryos of the seething human.
To adore is… to be absorbed in defined immensity,
to offer oneself to the fire…
and to give of one's deepest to that whose
depth has no end
as when Visigoths torched Basilica Aemilia
and coins through that bessemer
gushed over paving, searched its cracks,
and in the cool of a new sky jelled.

35

Or when they moved the capital
at the starting gun, before the hexagrams
had been invented on a prison floor
and sifted onto the wheel.
The Permian extinction has its mate stronger
from our own hand. That man's fire-dry
squint, cheeks gullied,
may I enlist as my lens, chilled from
having heard near the graves
as among stone chimeras on the plain at Fu-Tien
six marines cloaked in the rain practicing, gloves
cradling a box of air, the barked order:
Form up now, they are coming
and not judge eye-blink when lightning
commands because in frenzy
it explores entrance
into existence, we say,
searching the words dumbly, devout,
schist crumbling the fossil:
tendrils in and shines there,
its wavelength the mortal
red middle's although its amplitude lunges
beyond reach, foam
heaved from the bow.

36

Neither the gene nor the headache—
no single term determined my heading, rather the whole web
and so I was facing the writer of prescriptions
who left medical practice to care for his wheel-chaired wife.
His pad nowhere at hand and the cause everywhere
as he peers through it asking, *what does that white bread MEAN?*
In the dream that came to Brother Eustachius,
bread from the House baker Brother Ruoprecht
for their sudden guest, the naked boy. The entire Dominican band
circled him gawking.
Meister Eckhart recorded that dream when he was Vicar General
inspecting the Paris chapter.
Eighteen Episcopalians facing the Outer Banks near Kitty Hawk
were peopling my heretic retreat on the labyrinthine way.
White as perfect, the child tells them, but also a simplex muchness.
The man who is no mental expert but can bake bread, acting
through heat while doing no harm, brings the medicine.
Which leaves nothing out—all colors reflected rather than pooled black,
though black inheres too, piggy-backing the luminous. 'Be teleios
as your engenderer is teleios,'—that's not your ordinary 'perfect,'
because the yeast in that situation inseminates
wraparound force: one sees in others the ever-alive.
Across the room his wife's hand dangled inches from his
through days of rain from an offshore low.

37

Resisting, caught, they held that dream, and it ate at them.
As for evil—my hand lifted
toward the fluorescent ceiling fixtures next day
just as the ranked bulbs shorted out.
No storm then: it was an exteriorization,
testifying to my incompleteness over sixty-five years.
That for all my looking, I saw not. That for all my haste,
I had taken my time when there is no time to take.
That I had discounted daemones, gods, and men, separately and together.
My drive back north began before sunrise.
Crossing into Virginia, a winking antenna pylon,
its lacework angles tapering into cloud: Notional National Radio
promised the postwar life of Mussolini's body.
Steel fretwork dissolving, red dots on-off in the cloud's hem,
from swamp up through mist. Near Richmond
the interview with il Professore came from another station
well into its coda, the 1957 burial by the family and his claque
stiffening their Caesarian arms over florals.
Harding, Coolidge, & Hoover coddled him, Morgan bankrolled him.
I refueled near Grapevine Bridge where Stonewall Jackson
rigged a new span and chased *the Unionists*
across the Chickahominy
during the Seven Days. The plate in Gardner's photographic sketchbook
poses a contingent over square piers of logs:

38

bullfrogs and mist drove the engineers half mad
and croakings drowned out the night wagons.
None of those trees knew they were notched for the ax.
One retreatant oversees and chases parolees.
His eyes during the sessions stab, soften.
More than the rest he approves my heresies.
And the doctor: *My wife and I had the same dream last night.*
And Emmy too. Just what is goin' on?
Past the fuel pumps banked pumpkins and produce
are backed by mums in the drizzle
rust red, banana, petals beaded.
Cold Harbor Unit dripped the brown federal sign.
Unionist yeast, that driving story line, at enormous cost
to every member of the family. Fredericksburg and Chancellorsville
are fenced by strip malls up the corridor between the two capitals.
A wrong turn swung me past the Pentagon, the obelisk.
The Professore radioed again, now in mid-exposition
about the cult utility of the lynched, hacked-at corpse
at a Milano gas station trussed at the heels by his people
impure, imperfect, unsimple, to birth their republic.
Near Gettysburg a third station scheduled this before dinner,
the neofascisti disinterring him for the postwar elections
and the regime stealing him back,
salting him away until the tomba and the obsequies.

39

From Little Round Top to the Wheat Field no tree was left standing.
The idea in acting so as to work no harm
is to sense how plenum allows this in full push and rollover
while you gauge the opening and meet it as heart and engineer.
Returning dead are not shown, Arab dead go uncounted.
Garden of gardens from Sumer to Kew buzz-cut, two nations
do not need the same dream to share the same nightmare.
My wrong turn swept me around the gray Maypole:
vaporous through drizzle, topped by a Klan hood,
it faces a black obelisk in Iraq, for Shalmeneser the Third, suzerain
over five kingdoms including Israel—faces it
through two crossbow slits in its pyramidal cap,
as a yellow school bus cuts in, a boy clowning at its rear door,
Winslow Homer's in the schoolyard Whip
now penned up, *Alert* at permanent Yellow.
To catch desperation in failing empery
one must ride with the agent powers
day and night, in the high cabs of the big rigs.
Along the Appalachian night ridge past Harrisburg
a cantor and commentator together do Yom Kippur
while cargo trucks billow spume from the drenched multilane
passing each other downgrade, lightbars floating.
That day seals the knowledge disclosed nine days earlier
of who shall live and who die and how they will do so:

40

those nine days are the oven whose door gapes to yield
the aroma of the whole.
From the wheelchair arm her hand moves to his as to fresh bread.
The idea: that although no description of a system
can yield predictive understanding, a particular action
may still trigger in some keen radar-carrier,
gardener or potter or nurse,
the drift of the whole outcome and deposit it, the offload
of intact totality breathing and unharmed.
Morgan fattened the body but the partisans baked it.
In a Catholic country where burial goes by rote and bookmark,
to stow the delictum in a bag in a freezer in a cellar
calls for subversive tact.
And the ox's blood-draining dangle, he had to go that way.
Regression of force down the veins of unraveling system.
But now the cadaverous comeback.
As it must, being one of the permanent solutions.
Amber-dot quilted steel rectangles cleared each other at thirty inches
slowly overtaken at seventy miles an hour,
cold steam spurting around them, fuming
their tall rear doors. Tandem lunges, singular perseveration.
As the doors of compassion shut for another cycle,
nasaled the commentator, the assembly topples forward:
Open the gates for us even as they are closing!

41

The Hebrew for this croons both love song and threnody.
My hands cramping the wheel to sharpen my focus
on the spray-blown rigs, I turned Neolithic in a steel crate
yet heard anew behind the cantor, heat pushing it,
the breath of the line furnace under my Father
which, if they turned it off, would dump
all their hot metal into sand. Midway up that stack he hangs
in a bosun's chair adjusting sensors under the scrubbers.
Stripped, pouching tools in a chest sling, goggled
and talking to the riggers by radio. They begin winching.
His body has swollen and stiffened in the updraft.
Head and shoulders make it while front and back scrape sooty chines.
He stops them, they consult, he roasts, winching resumes.
EOS the dawn, bulletin from twenty-one doctors of the planet,
forecasts irreversible speed-up past the Eemium temperature maximum
from their tiny crystal set in the universities,
three pages with insets of the Arctic toupé shrinking
while the Greenland ice sheet makes for the shore
not at one foot but one-hundred-thirteen per annum:
unbroken hum from the puddled steel flutters their voices
but he says *Go ahead anyway*
and they keep dragging him, tool pouch slung from one hand
through the Holocene envelope for farming and cities
where ten thousand years shoot higher into the bore

42

out into blank straightaway.
The heat at Trinity was immediate,
flushing their faces at eighteen thousand yards
co-ordinate with the flash, well before any sound
and then in three minutes came sunrise.
That summer at Presque Isle
The black marks glisten as he comes from the water.
They could save their raw steel that time, and there he is,
he sunbathes on a beach towel, they have found their Jonah
and can dispatch him to the twenty-one elders, they can
disregard runaway feedback,
they have opened a door between unidirectional drivers,
unilateral albedo shatterings, permafrost forcings, sheet breakups,
have tunneled the tundra's methane reek and are going home.
Heading for the old Heimat, time for time-out,
they live to linger, they await Fred Rogers:
Mister Rogers the former pastor in TV cardigan,
to invite children back to their chairs in the neighborhood, to sing,
re-runs pressing on into early fall,
then two summers on into Lebanon-Guernica,
the president on trek bike ahead of Press, Secret Service,
yelling at max pedal up a Texas slope *Air assault!*
riding point because feeling unsurrounded clears his mind.
You're fine just as you are, yes you are, and I love you:

43

Fred Rogers slides as the meditative snake
from piano to blackboard to kitchen towel sneaker-shod,
Hermes of refuge for foundlings lost at home,
lilting Pittsburghese with the tear-wise eyes
of Fred Austerlitz from Omaha, Fred Astaire that is,
the two Freds cantors of shuffle and click, sweater and tux
to children alone anywhere as they feel the gates open
even as the gig closes, walking stick snatched from the air
and sponge ball caught on the bounce, the child or the rogue shifter
within emissaries from the child,
the vast ring of watchers liberated even as the gate shuts.
Exquisite timing:
the strong man in uniform returns embalmed at the party
just when broad-brush murder alone can no longer decide
the long game. Other powers, other dominations: so the pop-up returns,
bemedaled glinting headache
pounding the air with its fist.
The squat river lighthouse on screw piles near the Roanoke
carries in its cupola a single yellow one-hundred-watt bulb.
The millionaire who tried to salvage its ruined prototype near the Sound
sank two barges in the attempt, torching flotsam mid-river.
Real body gone, this replica was crafted and poises
over an egress hatch from a tunnel boring three hundred feet
back to the Armistead House. Certain slaves came there.

44

A particular night packet slows, the hatch lifts,
the screw reverses, an inky form wades and swims.
In one version it hoots, but that is South Carolina legend.
None of it simple. And still half-baked, still fizzed
by the muscled yeast, capital's chesty herald.
My other questioner, the parole officer's friend, sold his yacht last year,
feeling lighter now.
His eyes did not meet mine.
Looking again I watch him extend his hand, questioning.
Only the Sorrow Songs can float it, the havocing storm, the after-lashes.
In '43, Morris Graves painted it:
a fish rolled by the night sea
beneath a squat square of stars.
He also sketched her spread out on our plane,
hiving those four lights in her belly.
She, them, it, they heave and hold us
in the unsleeping sea,
our fluid gaze firm, our stand awash,
thus we behold them.
And I may inspect yellows in the rear-view mirror
only glancingly, the mums I am bringing to you.
Salvage is what the navigator manages as anthropology:
day that began in half dark, its tower a strut filigree
standing into low cloud blinking.

45

Spanos and Teilhard, Camus's recruits
and Nietzsche's squad on indefinite furlough—rebellion
was not the French master's advocacy,
nor was prophecy the pastor-son's willed ticket,
these were features of a face worn almost
as disguise to the general, seed husk cracking, and so
the child recruit, with the stretcher bearer hopping
trench spill with his loads, those young men do not die,
uniforms no protection, no definition,
one scribbling firily past his reach
by dugout wall, the other hearing himself called *baby*
like Budd, setting down that benediction in his memoir,
incredulous mustering-out by his own hand
as the first-born of terror in the presence-absence of terror
douched down by the fathers in three Dresden bombing runs.
The husk cracked silently, blindly
in Kafka's correction facility, the inheritors
grasping nothing of the order then passing.
Child: transmitted helplessly by Zarathustra on his wireless—
its precursors a camel loaded
helplessly through wastes, and a lion
scrabble-roaring through carnage.
That resolve humping, with that nerve clawing—thence their issue
the babe who creates: no pink sweetie.

46

The secure Malakoff of confidence
in young Melville's playroom, tower neither ivory nor sand,
but a sand tray: let the boy there harbor the man presaging his own exit,
inspector of customs on government pension entitled
by private right but also former service
to companionship in his study
by one adult who pledges to say nothing,
even of granddad commanding at Fort Stanwix.
Let them allow by that sand tray the law grow unhidden:
the tot's hand brings things from a table, musketed regimentals,
dromedary, bull elephant, cavalry blue, gray,
a farmhouse with piazza. Let the boy be the man
pushing customs papers then shaping five lines nightly,
a red flag over the try-works then a banner over the Shulamite.
Hours. The muting months. An unspeaking trapper-tracker,
one foot forward. His plump pouch.
The Malakoff, overrun, morphs into part of Paris.
Let allies, the irreversible alloys, gully the dunes of their bond
as black sails on Turner's Slave Ship,
repudiated even by Ruskin, float over fire
along one wall, Hawthorne dead thirty years
but actually it is twenty-seven.
In the old hand the boy's browses the pieces,
his senior watcher-buddy betting with himself

47

which ones will experience election
and root in sand. His average has improved through decades,
tuned by feeling that boy-sailor's writer's father's hand
waiting, through nerve straps saddling the arch, for the command
Reef tight to the phalanges, ropey belaying pins
of choice. No toy armory of moltings: their destinator
patrols grit seas for those left
disposable by the unaccountable,
short of election on their low table then craned out
into battle, pasture, through the sprit-sail laundry
flapping the roof of Mar Saba; or, stranded, wallets jelled
Pompeian, eyes neither believing nor blind.
For even such marooning entails an apprenticeship
to the patience of volcanoes:
their seam-deep communion with squeamish iron
in its gush ruptures toward light,
as with Bonhoeffer one evening at Finkenwalde,
his resistance seminary, a few pupils listening
as he rolled out Chopin or Beethoven
but suddenly
beetled over the keys, hammering freely striking
for oil or jewels in their raw vein
religionless, unscripted. Confessional
and illegal. And abruptly departed.

48

One throw of the dice:
each eye a gouge
and hell
at last has been scoured out.
The wind's umbrage leaves littered
morning as its replete record,
yet prickily bettered: anything
stirring yields the secret, that quantities
go on whirring in combinations
from sheen faces of the dies,
through commotions singly entranced yet mutually
entangled down stairways of order firily.
Emblems: six faces
as in the hexagrams from China, shifting truces
in the micron wars between elementals, change being
what change restores.
Young Jess Collins, drafted onto
the Manhattan Project, dragged chains through plutonium manufacture,
the bomb used on his twenty-second birthday:
came thence a dream in '49 that in twenty-seven more years—'75—
it would bone the entire globe. He quit,
his weekend painting now his week, with scissors and paste
a moocher from the image hoard, his great aunt
the initiatrix, her kitchen table their surgery.

49

Twenty-seven: three nines,
three cats and their cool lives if lucky. But years as pains.
What is called *world* had creamed into isotopes,
three times nine hurled into the changes:
in the year that JFK and Krushchev unscrewed the hinges
and rehung the doors, he painted a ring dance
of eight girls backlit by sheens from the bomb plume,
the flared hair of one girl spreading a cousin flame.
Thus a ninth child—that field of muddy gold
akin to the hot thing revealed,
rising from those eight but seen by none of them,
yet not to be quit of easily: inaugural nine the step not yet taken,
hazily a growth indispensable to some root set.
And with that gesture Jess touched what had eluded him:
not the world's future but his own had exploded—
for *1975,* added in series, make birthday 22:
he was the dream's target, it plumed his own ground.
Thus the hard inference, the hardest
in a life or a work fully to ingest.
Clasping a key, an owl has buzzed those girls
and, pushed high toward us by the tumult
flattening its color, its shadowed face is now the vault
of what had been and will be
clockwise turning with joined hands

50

into the one next necessary step,
world with an end. For circuit breakers fizz in the cells,
my own hells smelted for fresh trials,
each churning scrum eased to a ring dance,
chirping cries scissoring into the roar.
Not sentiment but sensing through clashed urges,
not love but cadenced intent, by the numbers!—and we
inconsequential yet entrained, out of tune yet keyed
over a fretboard's partials. The chemist who sifts
these unstudied square-dance pours
apprentices himself to the ways
of the girl at Enna combing fingers through field flowers,
at play but also in play—
abandoned there, thus mightily available
to a great aim and seized by it,
abandon as win-or-lose, appetite hung through wave ripple,
Ocean's tots paddling with her—
then she darkly queened over seasons, souls:
in this immaculate field we shall plant only
our shadowed Kore's white/black throw-weight,
prototype of the gaze
of the last Adélie penguin on Torgersen,
at attention on the rim indigo
of long nights, short days.

51

Vietnam: may the induration of our outrages
never wear smooth! Though our fathers anointed the orders,
guilt is not collective: each of us chose our own
tumbleshoot from the swept-wing
anus around us then, silver deafening shite poke—
naked, uniformed; feigning, fleeing; conscripted, proscribed.
Merwin vomited his prize back, Auden rebuked him.
Whereas at twenty-five Saul Bellow kept from his father
his dead mother's insurance payout:
I said, I'm going to Mexico. I don't know why I said that.
As self-styled journalists he and Passin
got an appointment with Trotsky.
At Trotsky's villa they were sent to the hospital.
The desk sent them to Trotsky's room minutes late.
It was 1940 and *his white beard was full of blood,*
who had said, Nyet, no worker's state invades Finnland.
The young man knew: there was no stopping that war
but there remained a theoretical question to be decided.
Getting which, he got to see that fathers
can decide, and pay. And that a son then discovers
why he has kept his appointment.
Thus the river: two men in a boat must cross it with one heart,
but on revolutions Doderer reminds: they leave
the abandoned, highly concrete task of one's own life.

52

Hölderlin in West Hartford:
they say they saw him when geese wrinkled low sky with honkings—
Mars at halt on the great wheel, he, stooped in morning coat
ranging between pool and garden
with a mute girl held back from school: something elate
in the blank stare, even without Greeks clawing past Turks
to stoke memory with combustion.
Yet the comma shape of his back and forth on slow boot
may be Antigone's push
past constraint, her virtuoso burn
through the stratosphere, *Vaterland, Griechenland, Deutscher!*
Cincinnati, Syracuse, Rome among bosky lakes, the burned-over acres,
high noon down all the roads.
Rumor has it that he's raging this time, that he's bats:
that he saw Diotima as Audrey Hepburn gassing herself
with eight limousines in *Sabrina*—who will support him, this guest
who teaches only how she died?
Conjunctions here bank the lightning, the upper room stilled,
suns rolled inside—*it soothes, here and there, the fire*—
alphorn suspensions shaving
these late lawns, high E-flat
over spectral Berlin and actual Washington
and the good place between all the cracks, sucking
the glaze tight, creaming the salt-bright screen.

53

Crossing Grand Central's lower-level scrum
to and from trains,
a jackhammer prelude by Bach, then
its source: gauntly fierce
over his wired keyboard while eyeing me
in need but dealing a full hand,
the black stare retroactive
past false boundaries on reality,
those destinations in lit letters
at the gates. Momentum took me past him,
those hands plucking at the seams
in the German's playful fabric
of uproar with law raucous where most righteous,
hooking in colder life
as the drag and drench of a swell caving to cream off
in low hissings, power-still.
Boundaries not holding in that assault wave
up risers at both ends of the cavern,
doubled ladder of no-path
to the undead, sought or unsought—
cold-chasm incense from his shredder
with me into day: sun, sun,
a gimlet's pick-lock spark
hanging hot flat and round across sky.

54

Point-origin fire unreachably eating itself:
I'm out from under the cool zodiac ceiling in there
(they painted it backwards),
faint slurring of shoes and voices.
His buccaneer agitato recital is not for us—
not intended to hold us—
but instead stipulates a Green-Card nanny transiting
that hall, our time's half-acknowledged Hagar,
the fragrant final wife. Who is unstoppable.
For territory is not ground   *terribilis est locus iste*
and may the end stand not as end but as goal.
To make anything in that time was to kiss risk
across darks, lip to lip telepathic   before suns lobbed
their low winter arcs, mortar rounds
prying at the far margin.
Was one tower hers, mine the other, sheaths sealed black?—
was that how the transmissions carried.
In architectures of fire shiver the architectures of wine,
tents of the drinkers of wind,
tabernacle in sirocco,
twenty miles at most to cool caelum.
Nor deathlessly does a country lawyer
yoke frequency with location
hot at the heart of the unseen.

55

For if immortality has currency
it has to be now: the lost chance improbably
draping fragrance down the lip
of a noiseless Bridal Veil Falls mid-bedroom,
my sight stitching jade blots through it—
no night-bloomer ghosting back, but studs
piercing wide batting, the not-done and the well-done
quilted through each other
buoyantly in a judgment
remanding life to convicted wonder.
Totality acquires fluency
even so: meat in flower even thus, spotty
to mitigate proud harshness—facing the meat hook,
Father Delp stood for *man as such* in the *sloppiness*
of a renewal that escapes measurement.
Breve enim satis, life short but sure is life enough
budding where guard is down
to draw my blear face my slit stem my prong
as secretins unjamming cracks in fate: the total
neither responds to questioning nor oozes clemency
nor dispenses the king's touch
but pursues itself in the round, a plenum
that works at not working while coming
to a crest here, here, and here.

56

A populist art aristocratically served
searches fraternity as it retakes the opened world.
The war in Florence is ending. Rossellini
deploys Sicilian, Neapolitan, Italian, German, Brit and Yank English,
as Tolstoy wove French, court Russian, Little Russian, and German—
a wounded Florentine doctor and American nurse (who sounds British)
thread through ruckus to reach
a wounded partisan leader in the hills. Against advice
they run the passage over the Uffizi
ducking its oblong openings. No crossfire comes,
sun angling parallelograms down the floor.
Gliding in front of them and carrying us, all still naive—
(she loves the *Lupo;* secretly his objective is family)
and they not knowing that a partisan will die because the doctor
will suddenly bolt for home—
the big Tolstoyan camera dolleys backward
into hazard, drawing the half-met pair
through the corridor where Thucydides and Jefferson
wedged democracy into oligarchy
and stranded it, out among statuary in tall crates
where the man and woman pause to scout their costly desires.
Which is where my accounting halts them,
though it will come. Everyone's breakout. But not now.

57

Azalea litter, purpurea against ground's
darker light: not the cruelest calends
but the best effort earth makes in time
therefore most dangerous and loveliest,
five-petaled hue of pain ratcheted bright,
necessary as home to sheer errancy
blown tissue thin, the one effort
quintessential once it goes unsupported
from the human bud: toxin
matured slowly out of its fuse to ripples
through heat, greater heat.
So the interior of that stable, shadowy rumples
on a flattened groom's jerkin—
you don't go asking about pattern recognition
when it's the whole relay
that will click you home or at last beach you
past the tide line. Beaching beyond. So, the shapes
remind you of Tintoretto?
Mary clasping Elizabeth in the visitation,
identical crumples of red with a bright zig between,
while I see Turner's scarfing shower arching
Fingal's cave on Staffa, steamer trailing its veil
sooty then ghost-bright over cliffs—
right. The known factors. But then there's that horse.

58

Cardano, doctoring the mighty, got out of town
instead of treating doomed
little Boromeo (lash that mule)—the same
who kicked him in his dream
for his lust after fees. Horny
hooves of the sterile as fruitful:
a tiny wrinkle greatens to a swell, grinds sand:
and it is dangerous to speak of one's own time
horizon wide, vast past its bulge rim,
the illimitable at home only with itself,
Ab o hawa, air at home with air, sea with sea.
Enter in there, with your diagnosis?
Lewis and Clark bartered dearly for their mounts
from the Shoshone, their companion
Sahcahgarweah finding her lost brother in that chief
and they ate horse in the Bitterroot drifts
and her presence said to all: these men mean well.
Homeward, it was Gibbons Pass
then Bozeman, known to her alone in that party,
notches into Yellowstone
she already at home, the others daring entrance
that they might regain home
and with it the laboratory of a stunned cranium
as the ablative absolute of search.

59

Colubris, snakey jabs, hovering attentiveness,
each ruby-bibbed blisser at the feeder
is named for *Archilochus*, no on-screen missiles
in a Long Beach room zipping toward drifting cross hairs.
Our classifier chose the man who threw down his shield
and buzzed off to fight again. Thirsty—
tilted pipette poking into a sky tanker
while the city awaits the thinker who will untie
its knot, not that it cares—
over penthouse and hovel temperature readings
slim then bulge the heat-seeking names. Yet that man dozes
in my bed, past his ear the Satanaël
shining there with the Light Man blurry then gone.
Our classifier melded contraries, serpent
through unwalled seas,
propellers roiling a burning world. *Fly*, croons
the imp demon—*Burrow, Baby*, growls the lump.
Ungovernably stocking the days as taverns, summer's liquors
bisque a glaze humping winter.
I parry the bare-assed hoplite poet, repouring his steel
down my strokes and curves. Is it real,
this counter-position I'm living? Unquestionable, his red splash
and my passion imploding to score
against him. I too am Paleolithic. And this is my war.

60

We buried the soul doctor in April's parsley foliage,
formerly engineer whose first job came
when a new partition at M. I. T. stopped his access
to caves under the Infinite Corridor.
TOP SECRET in stencil with a taped scrap
Help Wanted. The great I. I. Rabi opened:
—*What are you doing here!*
—*Your note here.* —*What have you done?* —*Built ham radios.*
—*Can you solder?* The first man hired
on the aircraft radar project, strapped into dive bombers
pulling up yards from the surface
as their fish flew crammed with gizmo cannisters.
Patients said he listened as no one else did.
Mind crumbling, he burrowed in cross-species genetics:
Most of life shares the same wiring,
and the switchgear in the wires, THAT's what decides
to make a worm or a Red Tail. So IT is evolving.
Us, then? One woman said that he held up
a picture from the alchemy tracts and asked her,
or asked the pitch swamp in her, *Is this what it's like?*
And that was their only converse that session.
Rope bridge materializing cross-chasm,
furnace heat below, and the join sliding back into hand.

61

So I could not ask him about Kinshasa, Congo,
the pick-up symphony orchestra & chorus
trained by a former airline pilot
who at first read no music,
instruments donated, voice trainers
from the Staatskapelle
coaching those walking in miles from shanties.
That is, ask him if all that
leapfrogged the switchgear. His daughter-in-law
led out the B-minor Prelude by Bach
on a slightly out-of-tune grand at the Friends' Meeting,
lettuce-fresh arrays
through windows holding the whole foliation.
That night a swarm of assistants
helped me thatch eight-by-eights,
wormy scarfed rafters, oak joists, sand bags, straw:
Berlin—not the recent end-time,
but one of the new ones, and we working
against time to stay on time,
to roof the Opera House with a mandala
of rubble before the fact.
The crumple effect of the full crescendo.
Patting, thrusting, completing.
From here, from everywhere, the same bombs.

62

The *Opernhaus*: down there in blue-white baths
and swiveling spots
the Amfortas wound reopens, and Faust wagers everything
on impossible odds, and Forster prunes
Billy Budd to the fable
it nearly accommodates, Cold War cold meats
and Britten helpless to save
Melville from being reinterred. Vere
like Pilate won't second-guess fate. Opera,
the opus, the job: so my part is to buffer it
overhead with salvage, straw, shards, torqued oak and teak
not yet riddled with dry rot.
At least the downbeat got it: the dialect of order
in the tone of whips. Caulk my gilded showcase of feeling
with pillowed apotropaic ruin:
not the Passover smutch of blood, but a compressed
strategy of extremes, raddled Schuld as shield
forefending the bads with a charm sackie
of bone bits, ragwort, beetle husk,
T s c h u k t s c h u k b e u t e l hung from a doorjamb—
while from bomb-bays my droning load
aims at my one chance
to stage what barely suffices
though still it enacts what I must.

63

Iris Cutting—Iris Origo—the Marchesa
young and green in the Val d'Orcia shale dry
on heights facing
the Kilimanjaro cone of Amiata
catafalque pale: Italy
punching its ticket on the black-boot express
and settling back, modern, primitive,
for the ride. She had one thing
I too have: the joyous discovery
that I stand a chance with grammar
only if the poetry is read aloud
by someone who got there the same way.
None the less even greater voices are no sure protection
in the accelerating rehearsal,
left hand following the line, right hand
timing beat and cadence, even injustice
leaning forward in its seat to hear, maybe even
to be penetrated.
The young Marchesa, who survived
iceberg Berenson, was herself
held at arm's length
by Tuscan peasant women,
try as she might to accept their hens, cheese, & silent smiling
while she caroled in Florentine.

64

The tall Marchesa had not yet written her books,
apron at day's end soiled
floating their fatigue,
but their own fruits, greens, meat
met their toil, and peacock-strutting flourishes
by local officials in swart
outfits Roman & Rinascimento,
that folly ornamenting hard labor
in adamantine terrain,
pitched her forward into
integrity: not yet the refugees
streaming up-valley from Rome, '43,
nor her resistance courier runs there,
but a first opening through
mirroring fate: fifty half-literate children,
she the once lonely child sitting her horse
or apart in the Villa Medici, half-orphaned,
now with a few outbuildings
facing the gate at La Foce,
making a school; carts to bring them, and their own garden,
meals, potted plants.
And then her own library, for her own books. And slowly,
the perception: descent real and underway,
this newest chapter the oldest of fights.

65

Concepts alone, empty: percepts without mind, dumb—
(Goethe over his roast beef).
The Navajo fire dance lends no immunity patch,
even the stranger voices through my belfry
bear no witness to it,
yet without the idea of it I could not manage
the undercurrent of random brutality
here, in this *peculiar fate* among my tribe
sentimental, at times cruel, coercive:
skillful in angling Cessnas into the Las Conchas smoke plume,
columns of gas torching and flashing a mile plus
into the six-mile updraft, some falling back,
stubby brands flicked over shoulder,
fuel depleted and thus yanking the needles on Ponderosa
stiff in the oxy-starved blast,
a wide glade of nails.
Hopkins remote as Pindar through the superheated
life cloud, ignitions unfolding into act,
clang weave through fate grist, *dragonflies draw flame—*
fury spent and we stand just here. Look from apsaras
swaying in the reliefs at Angkor
to dragonflies hazing the canals.
Look to your hand: the lines dealt there,
grip eased, the fathers veining its void sensing.

66

The guck lees of this shared lifetime
as sunny dust will fertilize what shoots? May I be forgiven
an involuntary back-glance:
Hans and Sophie Scholl fling their last leaflets over
the university balustrade, Munich,
caught by the janitor,
within the year copies streaming
from allied bombers, the winners
innovating the updrafts at Dresden
those same six miles, so that when Professor Huber
flogged texts on folk songs and Leibniz in his cell,
his ace opus was already out,
trailing his doomed students but signaling to the generations:
wolf howl and goose honk will save you from your abstractions
and also from these iron birds.
His trembling indignation, his gimp's roll, like Noah's,
set the pitch-perfect lodging of whole peoples
in the whirling gasket of times and pre-established harmony.
A limp swings off the whole body's impress,
tuning fork ponged into roving ground zero
by the bearer of imbalance. Across the courtyard
to the guillotine his trailing foot
nearly dropped its slipper—he stopped, snugged it
tighter, smiled to himself, and went.

67

The classic American Thermopylae
broke over Peekskill on Hudson
after the concert defiantly rescheduled,*
Paul Robeson protected
by thirty thousand and heard, heard clearly—
the first performance having been scrubbed
after the Klan and the tabloids
had pepped up the rednecks and local bankers.
So if you go ahead, enacting the inchoate
new thing, if you do not abide by
the causalists in your nest—
who read your itchiness
as jealous, wanton, destructive,
that your wanting must be the wanting on their terms
perverted, sent downriver—
then you will get it good and hard.
Thirty thousand among millions is no standing committee.
As whale lice whelm the levels, microdrivers myrtle our dreams.
We are fingering no one's slide rule,
nor a rebel yell, but that same column of air
in a vibrato throat.
Fire does not grip the stick from a love of ash.
Give me hands, feet, heart. Give me new skin.

*The concert by Paul Robeson & Pete Seeger, 1949

68

The immense releasing courage of caring hands,
two-way pulses on through,
something returns, but nothing wills that, palms outward,
thus in the ikon the lost horses
of stonemason martyrs Florus and Laurus
return to the pond
their dead owners gentling them, they gulping
from a second sky lips curled, arcs widening and crossing
through cloud resuming its blinding face
on the calm there.
Not the legend concerns me but this only,
joining the procession over Peekskill: shots in air,
stones, bats, pitchforks and two-by-fours, cars rocking—
stuffed down a well, caulked with dirt,
back come their bones commie and gnostic.
Rebel fragrance, riverbank at dusk
as twin manes pour
rewilding with water mutter,
tall in remise, nuzzling from pooled mercury—
seamless caring past pushbacks
and spurrings, the leap into clean loss by issuing
indefinite loans, father his daughter
moxie master his skills, mother her treasury even
void nursery of event.

69

You ask, said Applebaum, Johnny Appletree
of freed speech—the same old, ever old, rights fight—
you ask how this total information surveillance has affected my work?
I no longer have interesting conversations inside this country.
I no longer say anything interesting to my partner in bed.
Origo said of biography, that its kind of knowing
is like suddenly catching one's face in a mirror
and holding that impression—*a living face*—
taken by surprise but not prisoner. Very well:
only in '39 did her vagueness toward the regime register. By '43
hundreds of sprung prisoners, partisans, deserters. refugees
were streaming past La Foce or holing up
near Amiata, the Germans nearby. *As the menace*
tightens, all language shrinks to that of the peasants.
To Joan's apple tree in Bastien-Lepage, stool overturned
near her yarn-swift, as mute she turns from
her visions: one arm tranced among branches,
the other having dropped a needled
yarn ball at her feet. The pome grenade no one made,
Deuteronomy and Mark's baptism addressing *You are my Son*
to no one—that is, to everyone. The friend who brought this
came as Origo came to Bill Blewitt, out of the rain
with bread, milk, eggs, pointing to the next
dodgy perch. No one ahead of you. Immersion.

70

So the horse's turned head, rump twitching then calm,
stricken luminosity of the torch
in the crone's grip, idiot ease in the flattened
groom's body, rumpled
jerkin and cushioning cap with a face between
anonymity and singularity
do not point the way. Grien's entire encounter does that,
without a by-your-leave
and to blazing yet stripped ends: advent sans welcome,
enigma sans key, eksaiphanes: the sudden.
Whatever I have prefigured
must pass between a horse's tail, inverted torch,
and the torch in fact:
intelligence wall-eyed ready to flick it, or twitch
light from its fly-thrashing broom, brought on the run
to the altar dripping blood,
all vanishing like a lamp left on in daylight.
Out of dismay, amazement;
from ungrounding, sloshed earth;
disturbance the father, wonder the child, shrift
shaken not through levels but down zones
siphoning paternity from orphaned
minims, a nude throne
from no secured rule. Ungilded gleaming.

71

And so all that consternation
will sound off
with me accompanying it
on tambour, pipe, viola.
Even though it all comes
to a card trick
miming the grand show
cascading from cloaks of the senses
out to darks,
I take care for the unfolding
of either dealer's hand—
before tunes were, ears curled for them.
The front edge of elegy trims to aileron slipstreams,
ripple-mist into fadeout
over Andes, Orinoco,
an iguana's arroyo hide
from 60,000 feet.
The entire ball
drifts, a baking
cookie, peach fuzz,
green fudge.
It's alright to want to eat,
but it helps to know why you're hungry.

72

Thus focus and blur, hum and holler
web the interregnum stringing each nerve net:
ping feathering through ring fade,
through you but not yours,
fondue au fond on loan.
Through a wasp's goggles and a fawn's perked ears,
thrumming in a hare's cocked haunches,
rappelling up corn silk with seed,
the ground base of sensing
spins on aimed axles—Parmeneides
belted in with headphones, Empedokles scanning
the oscilloscope's trembly footers—
for the senses even in trance, freak, & swoon
drink steadily, since in their reservoir
pools the next necessary newness,
even as the twin cisterns, tipping, divulge
every content now, nothing you can do:
violet maroon vibraphone
in the snooze of our rumpled sty-warden,
his mounding codpiece
bedded on dung flake and straw
and so to sea-trench: sensus communis, inter alia
and across the kinds, out into ink
blotting between stars.

73

No, I can't help, I said. But need I have said it—
glistens rivering cheeks as she faced the oncoming
and me, our train pulling me blind backward.
Prajapati, progeny's duke, élan vital,
Lord of Spawn: the force of all that in every
upstart wavelength of being   *Drive, he sd* (Creeley), *More!* (Gompers),
They'll love you for it later (Underground Man)—
yet there, a closed fist, I sat.
Sun on a drenched sail steep frail solid for hours
as it dries, nearly humming—curving into the years,
her broken therefore her mightiest.
The naked degree to which I have brought together
in stable fashion, in the gray zone,
relentless opposites
as the under-genders of power?
In my last innings that portion still runs,
the auditors report, at forty percent.
Gray worn over the heart
hangs honest drab, but late April declares
that its pointilliste green haze
across still-visible trunks ignites marriage,
leaf bits flouncing staffs
of union, simplex
yet millioned, torched here and there with dogwood.

74

As goldfinches to leggy mustard, so patience,
miniscule pip, settles on the limit ranges
of seating in a chrysanthemum
out there in nosebleed heaven, the last tier
in Family Circle, mute point yet content:
being able to make out expressions on singers' faces
sans opera glasses by waiting on its power
to cup, fill, brim, tend, extend,
through its own valving it descends
past the front tier in that section, out over
the balcony, ranging down through steeper
inward progressions, defiles
canyon-wide, ridged mille-feuille with shade,
and exploratory it sways
side to side as the mid-range petals
take on size and snug in,
no one turning to look up, scale nearly life size,
the momentum wound by Kenyan runners swinging it
from a trail's opposing rims, speed greater
as the orchestra slides under, and Origo's
Only man is mad melts in the lights,
the center flocking somewhere past them among
sweating figures, the outered in-ness of all that
luminance. The populace of the bond.

75

Mums violet and magenta
by the armful into open ledgers
kept by the truck farmer on his dropped tailgate
write the balance: flesh severed
from broad spearhead clusters to flounce
memorial gatherings,
but once also in a doctor's office
where the patient, not knowing he would soon die,
had visited old friends
and the first settings of his mangled biography
arriving at what later proved
to be their last conference
with a cluster of red mums.
It's not spook omniscience, it's the appointment itself
that blossoms. A forward targeter
in a mortar platoon was out on the range when artillery
from another battalion mailed him
some unscheduled rounds
of bone-eating white phosphorous, and one came close
and by instinct he gunned his jeep toward it, not away
and for the first time he lived in slo-mo
as the white sprays
toppled near yet spun safely, ikebana,
down by the lake shore, shoka style from the dead.

76

In this marsh, flaunted carbuncle,
in this sough, a flagrant hand
proposing holy rankness
with slimes making for treasury,
for increase: in the unwalled basin
of distilled tarnish, a mirror
the thief chose not to take.
For though otherwise
a clean sweep, this stays:
soul that was truly seen, for brown safekeeping, soul
that saw it, for rosemary's rest in unknowing.
Neither deposit does one mess with
lest the great change not gather. Sinkings
brew spinings-forth, cumuli drift
through their spikes
building and unbuilding, all
inverted in earth: you did not
arrive here, sister, with either
the minnow's flash or a redwing's
raw piping, but the harsh grip of pattern
gracious then blindly splash-drabbed
beneath pines, a release
held at least this much longer,
silver sheathing burnt gold.

77

Like a camel
hauling its lifelong pile,
shitting itself in a cold hard stream
because wolf age pads around it—
this horizon in Hildegard's figure
shepherds my end. Yet wait, my December:
if I inherit only my actions, the rest
unstrapped and dumped, then those concretions
of my bad, good, and rangy in-betweens
will fill out the oasis, spread my cool intake
and the cud side to side in my jaw's creak—
the hairy tufts flouncing my knees
will decorate those acts
trailing dust skyward
as lifted ballerinas stream dry ice: stilting rump-first
to praise an unscripted sun,
day from a January nowhere on the freight ladings
yet scorching glory
across the freezing prospect, ice-hot
in the last wake-up
yet no haze there, a blast silent
and whole
through the worked-out hump
of my intent.

78

Gull fringing runway marsh,
half-belled cream over wave curls, your tendons brace
five pounds of balance free of my kind of hunger.
Seat belt snugging my little sun, engines
in massed glissando for strings and electric guitar
tilting up, their Heraklean hazing
and hounding craziness aimed—
through the climb into first fire I hear no first call,
each of us has been everything more than once,
even me running from Ares, though I was there.
And with the women. The question is not what grabbed me
and was I greater, nor whether the elders flash past
in a blur although steadying as blaze.
Tattered cotton, the shadow from each puff
trails at a hand span leaving
a little freighter, its winches, its unseen men,
labor looking to its own performance. May I come down
to what I have really done?
Acceptance, not the boot-heel thrust of attitude
or cufflink glitter of moral clasp, it is
seeing it as it is whatever it is,
and through that wind sustaining itself inches above
the granular basis, nervy grasses.
Then the touching-down, then the attainment.

79

Lifting a sunken mirror
from ooze: such devotion to trawling
in spite of bottom-suck and seepage
thrusts me again into
animal seeking, a bricoleur
dripping mud from his shiny find, a wobbly
refoundation platter from séances
discus-heavy, my ampersand into fate.
Bricoleur, not entrepreneur: jiggling
a sliding cloud, tree, peering head.
A walled garden of looks held then unsealed.
That one-size-fits-all blow
to the stable boy
is the surprise pushed aside
by a larger one backing it:
no allegory of lust alone, the engraving,
or at least it lets in
the express train that shoots me
through tunnel mouth into lightest
rockings, vastness, and a flash
creasing the valley
past betrayals, longed for
in anguish and arrayed here, compactly
floating nearly within reach.

80

Attention unflagging, lay-backs forbidden,
who will sustain it?
And the ache of last entrance, intimations
nostril-thin at feast and on waking, who curries
those fibrillations?
Yet animal earliness, the prime load-bearing
snort-flutter in it,
cellular integrals nerving out from it
to the sea's mass tilting dawn:
young Buber thrilled to, and as a man theorized,
all this as the supremely
other. Combing the mane of his first horse,
rubbing its hot pelt
with his palm, he had felt happiness lift that hand
through estrangement
into a freeze-frame around might, a power he feared
thereby forestalling his bonding to the clairaudient,
path-finding
foreknowing
night & ghost-reading partner
that stands browsing there also.
To mind in the hand's further grasp.
In collision may I call back the hollows in which
I never made contact.
In the cold, the high place, stripped down, may I remember
touching, being touched.

81

And so they have determined: Melville
frequented both wavelengths, transmuting
the gender-bending Q factor
with sliding bare instep along yardarm cable
sagging to cradle manweight risk:
snug that reef tight yet ready to whip loose,
a gull's streaming excrement peripheral in the gaze
that holds the deck planking down there
minutely spray-kissed.
What saves stays closest though unmanifest—
no less real in the arcanum.
When Britten, Forster, and Crozier
have Billy carol mitzvah to Captain Vere
mutely musket-erect
as crew haul on rope and a form
swings offstage, then across
the eros of opera breathes the unnameable,
quid no sister art inveigles from incest
or stand-alone loyalty.
Past all the books defanging this man in age,
ignite the Turners near his late desk,
sold short even by Ruskin:
torches proleptic of martial law
grown lawless, reddening our uncounted faces.

82

Masters of the intelligible,
repeat it—I must time the intervals,
tell me once more: how, when the stammerer
was lifted untrembling into suffocation
at the signal, *a preconcerted dumb one,*
the ship recovering from its roll
on the swell, massed cannons and ordnance
retarding that motion to the pace
of a steam engine's rocker arm tilting
imperceptibly
from slide into stasis and his form taking
the blush of the dawn: tell the ponder-sway
of the hushed vessel again to go vertical
and cup that high brief gleam:
convey the pendulum harmonic of upright sleeving
in security post-Malakoff, post-Twin Towers, which,
irreparable, achieved its fit
category down through category, slotting
apotheosis into mass
and sucking the asymptote into its endless
bounding line—
which received what had gone up
and aligned it, on time and thus in time.
Or else blotted it: you tell me which.

83

Cinema is the balloon jaunt in *Andrei Rublev*,
a brief lift out of our abattoir then back
into it bumping, skidding.
The knife that cut it loose also waits for it: life.
And love that dare not hold its pitch, shaking the lineaments
of grapheme and great-throated curse,
blatancy in high-wattage grease paint, tessitura bunching
the entire fabric into one thrill:
no frilled collar or swirled gown but the garter
cinching an era's oblation of the sexual
polyvalence of power
to the monotheism of display—see it not
as a meaning unperformed but high-stepping
a spur at dawn up the spine of Anapurna
before curved rows of faces,
black conch cupping them in a medical amphitheater
when the paragon lifts a red scalpel
to punctuate Hobbes's thesis
that at Delphi the command *Know thyself*
grommets transcendence into physical mechanics,
vulnerability the very
form of the state: wisdom forever off-key
yet richly vibrato stands face to face,
across the timpani and string basses, with life.

84

Baby Budd grows again—
fearing the woman in himself, he enlists, manning up,
then finds the gunship video,
but Vere is nowhere, to clasp him in chambers
with cracking heart home.
On leave, cross-dressing for the first time, he leaks things—
the emotion of singularity flung toward multitude,
both gobs at once reeking into the center.
Where fathers, by holding on, might have manned up.
But the gripped center has never held:
force brokers clamber into its sun ball,
that dazzle dot,
drafted into the furnace
past any fables. No stamen clotted
with bumbles, but a turbine's blurred axle
or a steam field's fumaroles,
slurries blurping queasy surge and relapse,
not roars of the dead
nor the percolation inside merit.
Which merit itself never hears.
For merit stays on the move: the moon's creeping
twi-beauty flush into and out of
day pulse night pulse coldly sluicing the marshes.

85 / *quantum*

Strategos kai poimen, commissar-as-shepherd:
a morale keeper, not some red Napoleon,
that was Chief Joseph speaking to Edward Curtis
on the record. Others had handled the tactics.
The photographer with a sixth-grade education
he could talk to; that one did not blink, he listened.
There is every chance
that I must learn erasure, amnesia even,
to reach the coppery imagos of rinsed
testimony: get behind myself
with the curiosity of the pre-dawn
while not hankering after morning knowledge,
an anthropology through and beyond tears
for early anthropos scoped out into end-stage—
nurse-quartermaster Joseph
already the general of fury worn to fatigue,
beneath horizons. For there first-light treads
under the rim,
emotion motionless as it moves, take care
only if you can take it, the care carrying
itself there as legendary Moses and Gregory
sped as blurry milestones
on no map, nor calendar,
running in place.

85a / *wave*

[*The sound is fading away, it is of five sounds, freedom*
the sound is fading away, it is of five sounds
and what this Ojibway song accomplishes
is beyond analysis (Winters). Thus
the mind in it eludes us, or waits on ahead.
Three sounds reach me, they are of crossings:
one sound is flowing away, it curls window-high, Florence
in flood, a gondola on patrol.
One sound shushes and melts, it is of two, four, eight sounds,
panthers in tidal sands, the pre-dawn.
One sound is coming apart, it is forty sounds, black freedom,
a tinkling shower, shattered skylight littering
see-through runes: Odin pats his flipped coat collar, satisfied
that the night over Svalbard will see
not Walton pushing his men across ice, but trooped hazes.
That the expeditionary bones, pitted like Gravneset Glacier,
will teem with the horde's heat.
That my tinkling defenestration will grant me fresh air
by decapitating my Alpha
and threading on past Zed, in inky cold prior to defilements
and following the hunt. *Storm light, all unsent for.*
For images are to be flayed,
their meat eaten, their skins cured and worn,
even zeroed and oned and made current.]

86

The unknowable is more than the presently absent,
but a cartoon God always shows up—
not quite what deploys missiles as Rostropovich said
Shostakovich was deployed:
With the Eighth he showed us that we would not win,
not really win. In the Eleventh the trumpets play
a victory march that is no such thing.
I still taste clammy morning air
in the Corso Vittorio Emmanuele
when Hill's *Mystery of the Charity of Charles Péguy*
folded open at the news stand.
A flare above both their testaments, I in my hole
and the revolutions and Putsches re-boxed in theirs
through dawn-smog archives, quatrains sappered by beetroots
and still I stop before
the altruism that heaves us across the parapet
when we have not yet killed something in ourselves.
Not unknowable, simply unmet: in everyone
it turns and takes aim. Try holding your breath for more
than two minutes. And no chisel I know of
carved Giacometti's burning truck:
photographed by Gerda Taro in Spain,
and he did her headstone in Père Lachaise, destroyed
by the occupiers, compelling us to the unwanted

87

effort of seeing past
what, who, and where the missing one has seen—
Alberto truing his stone on a notch in the range
past Delphi, to steady the change, not eliminate it,
possibly yes, you have known that
and the freight may have shifted, the swerve gone
back in its box, you wrestling with the big vehicle
and the ventricles have come
back into Brahms's rhythms, but do you retain
the throttling squeeze as it came
around you?
        Her view of mourners
thronging the iron fence
at the morgue in Valencia
lips tight and lips parted, learners
in that dumb salience
of the first aerial mass bombings:
you see them yet they are far, and where is the frame
if you, still on deposit,
stand with the dead in their loomings?
Gerta Porhylle, to you Taro
killed at Brunete, focused on two Republican fighters
pushing to enter a burning house, its tall doors
jammed, those letters or bread locked in the pantry
streaming in smoke from roof tiles,

88

and then a truck from behind, its bed and cargo
gushing flame, the cabin a blowtorch, no one
there to say sum ergo,
her friend young Willy Brandt absent, and Capa—
the pace fast the wanting simply to track elusive
significance emerging from the bad chances
in a good fight gone massive and ungovernable.
For whatever took place in his *Palace at 4 A.M.*,
seeming to pertain, in no way is implicated—
pushing to get in, were they rescuing someone,
those fellows-in-arms dressed like bricklayers? Tiles fuming,
one window belches the vulpine rag of night
from the wall's rim: are they after their tools, piled rifles,
records of all the wars? Those doors twice their height.
No one in that field where the truck hugs its load,
tires intact side panels running board the fuel waiting
to explode. World fire in no forest
one can name, sere separateness
turning to fraternity then hurrying under those tarps
to feed it: it came, it comes, it is still to come—
sage muteness, a babe's blurt, the jagged
flaring continuum of depth
in advents of the heart:

89

thus Gertrud Kantorowicz, art historian, nurse,
Simmel's mistress, Stefan George's favorite,
pried Ernst Gundolf out of Dachau on princess bravado
not once showing her papers. Paved exodus for many:
this is the other Gerda,
thus late to the Swiss border taking old women, one making it
while she to Theresienstadt—this the fire
folded in, the beyond within rescue, this, Jewess Greek Grace
known for her light touch in every tight spot
nursing to the end in the camp, the *Iliad* by her bunk,
her Leica the last chorus from the *Helen*:
High powers hide, extracting the unthinkable from the hopeless
as through trackless snarls the god found a way, so too this fate.
Photographs freeze motion, simple piety stops short—
but then the wonderful word arrives: Avodah—service & travail,
for Abraham heard nothing, *man must listen to himself*
instead of listening for it.... You pay with your duress.
Already her discus thrower by Polykleitos
like Cézanne's apple bursts with containment
in a torn condition bare to new forces, dangers—
equally committed to two movements, the figure
need not surrender to either—this her f-stop on infinity:
she, swan Pavlova, flutter-breaks then glides,
each wild polarity curving its charge in.

90

Exploding luminescences of touch
grazing the phosphorous of contact
in wave slurry up sand slope, iodines
recombining in the guts of smell
at full volume rallantando—
I pledge to outstay the heaping and dissolving
of mass into sway and spread,
or baroque topplings upward, clod to cloud,
either motion draining
the sap from presence. Cold Morgan
coughed up funds for Curtis only when one print,
Mosa, Mojave girl, paint slashes down her cheeks,
hinted the Greek dare: infusion
into each being of the full surge reversed,
only that as the way of belonging to others,
for that must be a possibility:
not the cheat of coherence through units en masse
but going whole for the whole and bearing it, maybe going under.
The detective's daughter more than once in her sleep
is smeared with nitrogenous semen,
yet no manhunt: sunny sand sifts fathomless cold
through unwalled lock-ups
under ledge-long tidal hammers,
their cloud-bank heads on the last thermals, destined.

91 / *quantum*

Sluice it in such a way that the grit carries.
The expelled turns cleanser, each grain scours without brawn.
How easily turn wayward during
agonies: first, expulsion and reprieve
then a yammering demand
at which a rock's wellspring gushers, trailing them
in legend to the Gulf of Suez,
yet they institute it: rupture, Mach 3
in each desert-dragged step. Dynasties
breed it: breakout, ex hodos, *light out for the territory ahead*
as day hatches in night's breeder-reactor heart—
stone of beginning as the rolled-out end
unbunging all beginnings: *the Anointed One* for Paul—
no one's property and no single man,
across the firepan of stymie
crowding even final clarities
into tremors. Yet antinomian events remain
actual perceptions—
mythology calls for bomb-squad handling
or we get Superman art at the Mormon Museum
and I have fumbled much en route to my worktable,
no oasis there, no Pisgah,
beginning as beginning again, origo traded for a start-up,
the can opener for worlds in hand and then gone—

91a / *wave*

[The smogged capitals inscribe *an ineluctable & unsustainable*
complex in a movement of time, Machiavelli's *as if God existed*
paving over Bonhoeffer's *without God, continually standing before God,*
in Santayana's Europe: *love, of which there was very little,*
was supposed to be kindled by beauty, of which there was a great deal.
Pound's China as *our Greece*: will it tunnel the big wave,
ride the digitide, push the etymons to flower?
Laconically the Sorrow Songs and Coltrane span integrals,
costly, not "improvising" (James Baldwin), as the violin-maker
carve-curves the calculus $\int$ through maple
on either side of the bridge.
From the inside out nature aims past itself. If I could prove
that the home-run sky shot of justice
and the hardball slamming a catcher's mitt can elude capture
by the bully nations, then I might ascribe to Blake's corrosive hand
those scooping loops that reef the heights
to the tremor within nobility
under hoof pummelings of guilt: only thus, inscription.
I never know if I really admire a poem
until I write it longhand (Thom Gunn)—
and beached up the hissing sand slope, the hand's
pricking downstroke seethes
with sequins and spinning dimes
in remittance for dereliction and betrayal]

92

—instead the gray declaration
that civil war has ended
and the abject go now unshackled,
burden dispersed to be reconfigured,
miasma less acrid because general
in a titration plausibly sub-clinical:
now your business is to persist
by franking the lie: exuberance, forward thinking,
PEARLS means practical evidence about real-life situations,
your docket is to insist
on what is not so because it must be so:
you'd have to be a full-bore dolt
not to hear what is coming down:
it's your business under the drumhead, massed tympani,
celesta ding-dinging through the reverberations,
to swallow hard and enforce happiness
pointing to beauty welts on the backs
of women in the dance, Great Rift Valley,
undraped in their swirl
in order to be admired:
we have been too long at each other's throats,
the air hangs sulfuric
with complex promise and a simple task,
you damn well know your business.

93

No hurry in the surge
of their hands into right action's glove:
Colonel von Stauffenberg, imperial monarchist,
with Dante, imperial monarchist,
trudge goat paths or deposit the timed satchel
bypassing the moneyed republics,
conditioned mettle meeting conditioned evil
not on our terms. *Nein* and *niente da fare*
to furnishing means for insulating a quorum
in its drag-weight drift toward
showing just enough skin;
to qualifying as nominal quotient
of a once-numinous quid,
populous this side of breakout.
At least the Navajo Mountain Chant
gets fire to the people before cold falls.
Nein to nourishing quarter-horses
of the half-measure,
nothing doing as defender of the false peace,
affirmer of the guaranteed,
deliverer of those fleeing toward capture;
hallowers of warmth fading in the dead hand,
psalmists of crêpe novelties in the mort gage;
bestowers of an extinguished kiss;
coroners of the unlived.

94 / *wave*

Precautions are necessary
anywhere near the last riser
into centrum, that non-dimensional point
anchoring circle, palace mandala, and fire-dance—
four gates into furnace core
with the cardinal directions shooting out of it
(not just on the page where your childhood
compass tip pierced it)—
fear not worthlessness
but wedded beauty *and* power: only therewith immune
to the cyanide mass heap-bleachings for complicity,
crows over stream beds at dusk
in flashaway murmuration   *Yes we are black with it all*
but we plead not guilty, gone just like that!—
only therewith and beyond, climbers into the lotus
out of null, one thousand petals
(my family, my children, at hazard
are yours also at hazard: great root),
thus a forehead red dot, zero fuse of the Two Ways,
where Jan Smuts relents and issues his quit order
and the long sticks cease toppling oncoming ranks
of the silent bareheaded,
Char Madigan inhaling that same ozone—
Not to win out over them, but to win them over.

94a / *quantum*

[Precautions rip loose screaming over this town
of twenty thousand, for one day ninety thousand
in blue coastal Maine—five Navy Hornets for days,
five fingertips smearing and roaring
steep separations, swoops, thronged throats
across my study's roof-window where I hoist
the 'phone to transmit their message.
Plato taught conversation well past the catastrophe.
Yet still I'm like young Tolstoy
beside the family coach among fields, a wheel broken,
as a plume comes at them, Cossacks passing at gallop
How terrible! and then *How beautiful!*
You sluggard, Meno, powers are the additives of dull thunder.
They punch through my ceiling, corned feet,
glass and plaster searching the grass.
Through the rafters of Plato's unwritten teaching,
into Kasbahs cocooning the egg-void archetypes—
those, too, precautionary membranes
outlasting any apogee, condoms for decline—
for I must become my own sweat lodge,
its smoke hole covered with tissue paper
for me to crown through with my own heat.
Plaques at Harappa show them at it, full lotus—
war and peace *hip-hip!* out of bone cradles.]

95

How, then, to let it in—
not clambering at 6 Gs but here, unadmitted—
smooth-sheeted alcove, thalamos for powerlessness
accessing power, the deathless through dying:
Shakti letting it in from her Lord, humbuzz at all seams,
wide hips hauling their void open-eyed into perishing—
as if going through that high yellow antechamber
then to corridors with cameras, to the class of lifers:
my taste of Judith Williams's routine
through sally port, elevator with cam,
doors unlocking and relocking
until we're in the inner sanctum
and the men learn that she too has done time
both here and in Honduras
where a colleague crooned "Honey Bun" from *South Pacific*
and the guards eased back.
Back here, rape was her fear spell after spell,
as with the transgender woman in our line-crossing posse,
inviting our care should the guards pick her out.
Kodesh Hakodashim, hagios ton hagion, tall screen woven
with azure, scarlet, and violet guardians—
Wilmer's Greensleeves: *O my love is like an*
Out-of-tune ice-cream van
those as-if-dead killers alert on folding chairs.

96

Musical chairs among the resource lords
in gamings of denial
whereas I wait for the rod
swung by a wheeltapper—dull clanging
between the bogies to free brake lines
of steam crud, whirled sand and oil—
early desert morning between Durango and Feather River,
between Mantova and Venice: each time, the stroke hanging
Skimpy reality, wake, hurry   then in fade-out
Patience, long draw and single wing   *How is it not here if you suffer it*
and if you out-suffer it how is it stronger?
Elvie Thomas in the '20s spearheading the Blues
I got little bitty legs, keep up these noble thighs
then evangelical, no longer jumping trains—
endurance taking shelter stiffs it, yes, sky capping cliffs
in monuments and stillness.
Yet if remote electrons though juiced blanks jive in attunement,
then we too with the flywheel axle, both carrying,
Stilpon my physicist: omnia mea
mecum porto, salmon after their stream climb
in a deep eddy holding,
stippled missiles
long as an arm: I carry my load
and if I bear it then it will carry me.

97

A wartime literature, the scrapings of dog's cradle and mole's,
crystal-fretted from muck and the jells
of fledgling winter. Steam from snorts in the stalls,
nosebag unreplenished.
Years on my nightstand a Chinese turtle stirs, speckle strewing it,
gold-spindled stars on its sky shield.
Each morning, then, horny yet fertile the immobile whole seethes,
prehensile toes in the crawl stroke
of the hells liberated, deferral on the move.
The pinch of hopelessness stirs courage,
a stallion's kick shuttered within each bind,
Bernoulli's gravestone pricking the sight line:
Consistently rebooted, I arise.
Bloated on fetid straw and slimed water
he bucks with last voltage, alive to the men shot from him,
the clinking Frankish Following riding him in ribbons
sun-wise around their settlements, hooves belled and barbered.
Thus across atrocity and gimcrack at gallop, wall-eyed
through dusk forest: this also is to love height, and width,
and depth, and breadth, a knife seeking its sheath
in a dark room, and finding. This also,
though flies buzz his backbone. Only despised weakness
binds me recalcitrant to others: thus power,
two-faced creation that both advances and falls back.

98

Time was that Douglass fled to Canada, then London
Time was that Reverend Colonel Higginson said
Here am I, come get me   and no one came
and that was the same time, and both were its measures,
John Brown the lit match, they the two logs burning—
time has quality, tendency, aspect & aim,
has fallow and fullness twisting the same cable:
clocks it is not, nor term limits, nor smoke
from the snuffed wick,
Come get me   the glove to its hand,
throat for its kairos:
saturation in the cloud,
curl up the levee,
hands on thighs pushing down, spine towering.
Time-is fountaining from time-was
through no span other than its own
seen down the ladder, rippling your torqued shirt
as you turn there,
at stand in perilous whole light:
soaked sand beveling to lappings,
blue to pewter my hand's raised rivers
roll gargled pebbles there
with a boy's hand inside, he who played
still playing, thalasseousai.

99

When my grad-student office mate at Drofnats
pushed the door open and yelled *Give me that phone,*
they've shot him! slam—he called his wife,
then turning explained:
at Notecnirp he had been recruited into the Company.
They, *y-e-h-t* they, were behind Dallas.
One bonds with a forceful tutor instinctively.
My alliance though immediate
has remained unnerving, only now
threading like dribbled code toward
the rise of farming and cities
when *the whole-body perception of the animal*
(Paul Shepard) began to erode.
    When that door crashed inward
his command, its unencryptable blurt
from the human onset,
was a bear's clawing salmon from my grasp,
teeth a high chancel in his reared skull,
Nicholas von Flüe's Wotan
but this time no crooner, no hived syrup,
an incognito complicit Christ
for love of the clan but no longer the tribe, for the den
but against his teachers, mad now
for the held tone of truth.

100

On Princeton's midnight streets down the black middle
I patrolled with Clarence Brown—
Your daughter believes she is a midget. I've promised
to grind some growth powder. You've been forewarned!
and he could be relied on for contraband,
Mandelshtam's widow having stipulated
that the next interview would go more satisfactorily
if he came with a quart of mayonnaise,
for time hath flavor and aroma, post-catastrophe,
post-cardiac infarct. His cartooning pad marched blank squares,
rows of windows, past which Hitler strapped in a wheelchair
spun in free fall, arm cranked high,
and his charts of Mandelshtam's *drifts* in 1921-25—
teeming keenness clicketing rough shrill the shakes
prickles muffle-tucked in a haystack of dangers—
show all that profusion aiming
toward blood, not building but unbuilding
a commedia of spin-out, clown car disgorging still more cars
as greasy red grins pop out
prancing on straw and manure.
Thus with a door's mute pulse stagger and enter:
alone you could not have found such a path to poverty.
The trove must be ruins, the beast must stride clear, the way
open onto swept ground.

101

Both were hasty, Vere and Billy, *Baby* with man
each leaping the chasm, but Vere seeing down the line
of sacrifice and the aeons
quantum/wave, hard to hold, omnia mea porto—Pauli too saw
but hung back: the mercenary tinge in his feeling for women
provoked a dreamed Chinese nushi to confront him,
his plasmatomic Beatrice: *Push through unstammering,*
tell your guild, it's like THIS! He balked. Thus der Pauli Effekt in labs,
as now for the human experiment, spasming, seizing up.
It is you whom I study, Captain, as your womanly-mild foretopman
tongue-tied punches through your test case.
Vir, & Bili Buada the war-winning god, both perish
in order's ardor (as if a forehoof sprang
through his fist, Melville's Timoleon sleeved both powers.)
Moral rigor, and the whole body
an impacted verb, together strike through us to save
not the last animal but the first
unitary justicer, squall son as quantum father
quashing the ghoul. Quick now
where they passed separately.
And so on, until we get it down.
In my ace engineer Father's dream, hauled atop
an unfinished office tower at night, he quails before
sudden moonrise: *It filled the entire sky.*

102

Two brawny gravediggers: from one grief slot to the other
by long-handled spades flicked over-shoulder
they trade spill through neat arcs
as if from the prior dead to the oncoming dead—
with brusque tenderness toward the centuries
they stand through one more day yet from first fire—
their twined oaths ragging me for a dumb Johnny:
—Johann Ghat!   *—Jehanne Ghat!*
And where would such mated steps go down
past stripes in the dream of the weave of plaited order,
the skull's winter journey among summer lightnings
to a curb soaked smooth
gurgling *Enter*,
save under this rain, Jehanne,
drenching the seeming steadiness of place
here between stream chapters:
thus passes Hermes, thus Klaus's bear drips honey
along the chill smear of the asymptote,
that zip-line where Tyndale heard
one jott and one tyttle
            of the lawe shall not scape—
so take my hand: a stream there is,
though upstream into itself
here between everywhere through this
dear carney show-and-tell.

103

From trees mid-August miniscule slow rain,
swapped-out life with brown edges
swirling around ungreeted death on her ten-speed
ahead, pumping uphill, slo-mo estampie
enfilading yesterday's gone fire.
Turba and putrefaction in hollowed-out
calends and their malefic civics, even these fiestas
write no permits for deafness in the heart's piled tenements
window by window, a two-million-year-old lease,
ghats naming both the aeon-heaped peaks
and their strict passes—thus ashy ledges along Ganges
stretch floods to a taut thread miles high
pantingly, at a stand!
                    Long mêlée, strew me lightly
in service, that the small rain
dun can reign: it takes a brawler
sprawling to track that chalk-toed ballerina
returning yet always ahead, oscillating
as the fear feather from my spear's tip
wobbles at aim aiming,
or radar screens lighting up on Thule
with missiles from Siberia climbing over Norway
computers 99.9 per cent certain
though it was Luna rising
Don't take yore eyes offen her but don't grab for her neether.

104

Knowing her better than I know myself,
still, when Natasha Rostova shrieked—
the hare pinned, its red paw
thrown to his dog by old Uncle *Right you are!*—
that penetration of the whole
by elation out of sorrow into cloud pronged by blown grasses
and the thing bled to its milk lining day-lit,
my own secret absorbed on the meat wheel
as a priesthood by its sacrifice—
these as one joy toward the flung foot
clotted with dirt is how I would speak
my unutterable into the bessemer
of victory and extinguishing.
But first—and this down years
through sandy delay—there is the corridor
to a round chamber under black skylight
beaker where powers fizz
storm light, all unsent for
and the hurrying figure with me—
coat collar up, hat brim low, tell-tales north of reason—
toward the door he flung open
on a woman with her friends at table,
and seeing him she screamed keeling forward, the glass
toppling in, cold downrush and the cone of stars.

105

Late day: preparation for guests
soon to arrive has me at the customary
scurry muttering to myself,
yet this time clearing clutter without haste,
ice water beading glasses, screen door
sifting woodlot sibilance
across unpaved road. It is time.
And after a while past time: an odd peace
sifts me as I sense they will not be coming,
minutes expand—nothing of the old flurry:
such an inheritance to have come into
in my own rooms. Among the maples one trunk
reddens deep in the array, stem gleam
becoming all of orientation
for a long breath on the other side of is:
not as one axis growing still
but all of them, as in midsea swells,
their hung facets holding—
an undisclosable hospitality of everything
to everything else: now that I have let it go,
it can touch me—the many gone,
their ozone margin of departure,
the thick pass-pass of copresence, pausing
in mute wide welcome.

106

Bassani rose from tables at the Rome Academy
declaring to his wife mid-course: *J'ai faim,*
his voice in the film with Pasolini
on betrayals of the Postwar peace even cooler:
behind discernment, a distinct hunger
and distinctive taste.
For the living had already stood up among many dead
and looked around, brief aromas
of food reaching them
We are famished
and that was no utopian nonsense
nor envy of someone's table,
but uninventable appetite for completion
after abomination's push into broad day
micron against micron, hulk banging hulk
black white white black
in antimimon's roughhouse tribute
to the open-pit mine the Christ had gouged in the mind
from rim to rim hazed layers, storm systems
breeding flickers, delayed crackle—
the impatient righteous dead in John's bomb manual
(Patmos issue, prison or refugee dugout)
who are told to pipe down because still there must be, even so
a little more killing—

107

that tension wanting to play out
in the worst way—and it has—
across the dance floor and every plate laid at banquet:
a fight the brigadier cannot settle
until a supreme standoff among duties
has split him clawing, force within force
in the ripe conflict that duty is
when it remembers that its arrow
every time flees the backside of direction
and thus half the sky
(this way of putting it will seem gimcrack—and it is—
but it cleaves the *I* open to standstill).
When Lord Amherst's scout Robert Rogers
and his Seal Team for scrawny empire
pressed west of Montreal in winter at record pace,
he still without a commission, famous but in debt,
they paused before Lachine Rapids on the St. Lawrence,
standing waves that Cartier
had never seen the like of channeling force
through the surge, blotting any yell.
Reservoirs of transmission and treasuries of disturbance.
The cancellation of will happens: over one's head
an encompassing and more spacious
dimension, hungry, decides.

108

Groundless territory   *terribilis*
the squid's ink-clouds no veil
                    for Iscariot's chute into night
and may the goal stand without end,
a sentinel standing glad in his bones at night's close
amid signature strikes, target-template karma vaporizing
in praetorian karma: gone, Hadji Murad's great-grandsons
(scratchy phone video inadmissible as evidence
against those getting their story straight
digging bullets from bodies).
To make anything in that time was to make time
into a caravan trailer for thinking
suffering destination as postponement
or a border retreating ahead, behind which refuge
likewise can be no goal—
that nurse-inmate in Theresienstadt reading Homer
surpassing such measures: shame, then,
if I lament occasion for its opacity
when even it, wall sealed by daylight, can disclose
in its rubble core, its rabble strictness,
secreted dimensions:
opaque to eyesight, still, to one who looks,
a parch-bound unforeseen power: terse integer
that would touch me open
where last breakage kindles.

109

A swiftly oncoming deadline favors the live mind.
Cirrus-wide scope over jammed abattoirs
chokes my rucksack with skies, not my tasks. Nathan Hale
stiffed the colonel fresh from London playhouses
with Addison's *Cato*: *I regret that I have but one life…*
Yet if a sun pole to the dead welded not glory but foundation?
I'm no longer counting. *Only the mountain submerged in earth*
musters command. Only love past desire learns courage.
To study dusk's emotion, thrusting then dragged in surf,
tucking into the endless beneath a bat-clouded sky,
ruddy twitter-folds ruffling up through footlights—
where foam-slither down the ebb, the lethargy lethal in me
meets the inrush Christ-Hermes sparking there, crosscut through smash—
kerukion, ignition: remember something, anything
of what you were in the mountain.
Hand, off the tiller, floats on the main
feathering with cirrus.
And pastor-hellraiser Higginson
swam naked that night from his black regiment
a mile toward Port Royal, watching the Secesh
on their causeway, when a hound barked, and he turned
swimming long underwater, breaching
suspended between the two shores
through the counter-draw.

110

We did not begin as the Coriolanus
of all species. Smoke from clearings signaled
that our long prelims had ended,
but not that we would streak from partnership
with the eld, smashing the tempo of eld.
It's the isolatto
clamped around his outpost
in flooding wind past the campsite,
the fist of himself around the string board
of his spine, Strad viola out of its shoeshine-black case
propped in dust: it's that fellow,
not hunters nor the cornmeal klatsch
of singing wives, who cradles an olive-drab crank radio
gut wired to cortex
and hauls heart for the plenum.
And knows that all of this will be thrown over
for a sack of sprat gimmicks, sagging
with the throb of the entire tale.
Spindrift threads tremble the blown inlet, regimental:
against each, enfilading fire from both sides—
res publica as lace shawls on lucre's harbor?
good for reenactments, studious forward crumplings
wreathed in smoke—but no: vintage salvage, strung makeweights,
spun foam's thin heroism easing then tensing the line.

111

A gift from fate, no contrivance of effort,
a rock wall without pitons, abrupt rhino hide
where moss had baked in the strobe aeon of days:
there I leaned stilling panic
in sunset forest where I'd lost track, and now,
knowing I got out alive, my thin skill points to the hunt
as what will still meet our extreme need—
for, locked on quarry, the trance running that formed us
is not the running in dreams. Bolt-still against the malign chances
I hear *black ice childermas* I hear *unchilded at quick*
yet even so, oncomers, I'd have you be leveraged
by antelope thighs, so that you'd hear grasses
thrashing you with a mind of summer. So that finally
in you we'd not go astray.
            For only trackers playing their gambit
might lope unerringly
through *Mary's doll-house*, Chartres:
the builder's encircled hexagon, thrown, drove his big game
into a net of triangles, rectangles…
seven of nine spires built, yet nine choirs foresee them.
Even Mandelshtam's wasps sipped at earth's axis,
not at the eaves of his cathedrals—
thèir nave, fire-dinted darkness, hives the endless.
An arrowing buzz and sting are the yogas in hands
about to grasp their birthright.

112

You did not spokeshave the roof beams,
truss the tension frames,
though you felled grandfather
with axe-driven wedges and two-man saw,
unswaying tilt
to crunch in, great flail;
yours not the hand adjusting turnbuckles
with a pipe-fitter's wrench
on tendons sleeving into the joins
of plenum, habitude
arching from Haida Gwai to New Scotland,
Ailsa Rock to Peterhead,
Bergen to Spitzbergen in the known relays
fibering the quilt tufts of unknowns.
That blanket warming all and securing none.
That house whose door frame stands nowhere
and whose footers sink everywhere. Grand Opera,
opus magnum: not yours the full leasehold
120 days of Sodom 24 hours per diem
though you enjoy jostle space,
not yours the custody
though your wallet bulges with papers
and claims exerted by those papers
and receipts for the ammunition and the privileges.

113 / *wave*

A black Swallowtail taxis, flicks on his twin lanes
of landing lights, assesses
the fact that now he is both the aircraft
and the runway, folds his cards, and shudders.
I am the renegade holding pen for Bluefin
and I am the shears, for I grant to *I* release
through rupture. Menhaden row backward
whisshtt one more chamber of maiden thought
across ash-drifted knees, Shiva destroyer of worlds—
old pogy to the rub-out, oily mossbunker
backpedaling to ample childhoods in India
elephant-eared swaying, guzzling from mud
puddled gold at sunset
and one of them a tank commander at Third Wipers.
Thus combat chits he tied to a pigeon's leg
attained the loft in five minutes, while
an express train in a tunnel rolled unbroken
a huge passage with great doors slamming all around
as commander Bion put it. Elephant child,
skimmer sifter of the wave, its own fat as pan butter—
smallest fry in the sea the largest wager
and I shall be small among the small, in the wave acid quiet,
far cicada smithies slugging at the ring
of fading all-out effort.

113a / *quantum*

[Our blinkered wanderings through a defining sky: no hand-me-down,
hand-to-mouth zodiac quite pins it—
defining because bottomless and with least tone
as a struck cymbal goes on quivering:
no up and no down, yet stemming from there
all orientation (sunrise billioned)
which constantly finds us all the while it shiningly
shows up, the unbounded
funding the manifest.
And did the five pilots read this out of their instruments?
Did the gut punch of arrogance float sleeved,
did the fuse, the benzene ring, accommodate stymie
and scout the resonance chamber, did it all still fly for the community—
did they too peer past the disciplines
to the ur-phenomenon? Past sound and the animal look.
My views vanish, dead reckoning remains:
your acts will remember you.
Well, now, Meno, they used to be known for their money
and their sleek mounts.
The surge that rams your dread clean through you toward joy
pumps through ant and thistle
but in you also hangs amazed: such a place!—
shown and whole and present yet the crossing
unimaginable or forgotten.]

114

As if the woman most needed were grafted in,
her skill at deciphering old texts keen in me,
this time over panels in a farmstead museum—
folding out to a pudgy cross, worn finish
over red alien lettering
by some ancestor genius, likewise a woman—
my own line's lost fountainhead.
But I could decode nothing.
Outside, lakes ball-peened by midday.
In their crinklefire I entered
an empty armory
and I was Muir, who dreamed the great animals in procession,
gazes lifted in worship.
Slowly came red smears, almost a cross again,
hazy then sharp: forensic marks through legible
outlines,
      children. So, that
ageless abomination, even, even here, here: no weapons evident
for either doing it or preventing it.
Complicity would have been easier—
our whole experiment, self-canceled,
its drag finality in the last impress
of first things. Sighted woman within my blindness, I clasp you
not to quash revulsion but to hang on
where no holds grow. For you read me, you read me.

115

Oppenheimer dying grieved unlived theory,
Dyson came but the equations would not catch,
Dyson could only hold his hand.
The atheoretic life is unlivable.
Getting all those power shots in, their implementations—
instead *it is the stubborn desire to live*
looking for a way out   François Jacob on the prehistoric
trapeze swing through blackness
by dame theory: sheer need, thunder, solar storm.
Witch with a torch, no, for the dread kick met Oppy
as a diffuse blow: years of kudos,
the one extreme scenario excluded by all the calculations
laying him thus, that early seer of black holes.
Thus *equus* mates with the exiled, *das Schöne,*
the blood-flecked horsetail brought on the run to the haruspex
as Pound's, for he got there before Puhvel,
as Mandelshtam's, for his brokeback stallion lathers
our own dumb dust. With needles into its hide
they mark the slaughter lines.
Smothered, the ruling backbone, sky—him the queen lies with,
but whoever kills him, Varuna kills:
bound and unbound, yoked and unyoked, Svāhā!
squaring the circle, black suck permanently shooting
into itself, two iron omegas slamming totality.

116

The country that tortures openly has made
every law porous,
or pre-Greek, though they did it too.
And if one cannot trust someone absolutely—
even if one has been the betrayer—then
the very outline of feeling
contracts, you are less-than. The straw-flecked
flattened stable boy, he has been
busy tabulating this two-ended business
for more than four hundred years.
Older, the trespass, lighting fires along
the ranges in his piled lids.
One morning early at the Café Rex
in the working district, the air inside
went amber, crystalline
although everyone still read, ate, drank—
thus the feeling I had not yet
been able to warrant, for one woman but also
for my fifty years. Not rebirth, that mitzvah,
but an ending, a tulip tree's fat blossom
of gold milk cupped browning in dirt.
Arrival flipping to wayfaring—to have been at last
true yet topple helplessly
severed, ecstatic into deeper earth.

117

Over his desk Shostakovich hung *Nana*,
the doxie not by Manet but a friend, the blouse orange.
By '49, the Ninth shat upon, the Fourth Quartet banned—
Lesser compares those paintings and then the emotions
in movements two and four of the quartet:
tender then slightly monstrous, vital then fevered and anxious.
Hush, child, it's not kreplach, we roll the pastry just so,
then pinch it, add this meat, then the spice, see? No worries!
But I know: she'll fold it over and I'll yell *kreplach!*
Giggles morph into insight's bee-bee vomit,
the bind of the time sees through you to its own twist
and there you writhe while it is still it.
From the brothels of Manhattan Simon Magus trawled Sophia
in orange chiffon, still ignored,
Before the worlds were, I was—
though quiet, she will not rest, in the stable too it is
her flare over sprawled Gaston.
The horse gets it, but I have to work it out.
His tail paints that run to the high altar red,
gleam sliding off the motorcycle cops' blue liveries
in throng din fluttery, unmoving,
the pursuit of happin-… worn blurry, senseless,
off by one eighth of an aeon.
Orange gutters amber while she flees forward.

118

They sat me down, interrogated me,
asking what I had seen with eyes closed, and I said:
the honoraria of sadness nugget-bright,
ores ropey molten in the encased seam,
and messages, or messengers, their in-between
blood filamentals criss-crossing
pain-clear soothingly swift, at rest in
unassessable velocities across chiasms
chasmic in their embassies.
A slender babushka sat there too listening.
A steam train took us to stubble acres,
we got off at dusk,
early snow in the air. But paying up
is not just crossing a field, and those flakes
did not wet my face: a width of cessation,
neither to reach for nor shelter from
there in that field we were crossing. Midway
at a tub she stopped to pour from burlap, and nuthatches,
chickadees, wrens flocked her red-streaked scarf,
face by Pisanello, cowl by Millet,
Origo in there somewhere
with the simplicity that eluded her,
bearing by Piero di Cosimo
draped by Winslow Homer

119

and her lips didn't move yet,
it was me churning:
All these flakes, statistically different,
and they don't melt because
and here George Spencer Brown's maxim
floated to meet them:
The value of a call made again
is the value of the call.
Especially the unheeded ones.
The call made repeatedly without
quite replicating, that too would be the whole value
of an expansion culled from the call.
To flock, swarm-intelligence of the above
seething through the below—old white-beard again—
swarm-stitches the ant colony through nebulae.
And now it has me surfing under its comb,
a pull-saw huffing kerf and turpentine
down the back of my hand.
Here every severing
has emerged from error
without leaving behind false
generosity to myself.
And then she spoke:
Feed my birds.

120

Nosce te ipsum
not the hobby of an absentee God
but a quick blow to midriff or back of the head
that no one invents for oneself,
that no one sustains in joking address
to one's own sweating preterite, their heads
drummed by the uninvented,
uninventable ground bass to any imaginable
voicing of the confession:
I did not make this, not me the source, and yet
for this I am made so as to unmake illusion
and damned folly, deus
otherwise plasticene, deum trued
on my otherwise blind sighting notch, not
agnus dei but prior to that,
lights out in the stable
and in the skull and down in the engine room
a gurgling just past hearing, slosh majesty.
Though I do not see them and hear nothing,
they are all still there, they recuperate
ignition and extinguishing, they flare and snuff
every fuel simultaneously,
cover me over no more, this heat wraps me.

121

Pale gold corpse, sunny beech leaf
powers into the snowbank
Why this is Sodom, nor am I out of it (Kit Marlowe, mostly)
yet *heavenly living is now* (Swedenborg)—
slicing a line-drive for Thule,
one stab at squaring the circle of our crimes,
no raised hand quartering the seas in their font, no ring-dance yoga
of turning around oneself.
The 121st day, implausible vastness, pure gravy—
but no Kali in our kit, her necktie of skulls
rattling tutorial for annihilation
through our whole show: no waiting on remission of guilt,
no hand lifting into blue-gold, the human sky humming—
nor Magwitch clanging the crudded grail,
from girder thunder under bridges
over the little cook fires.
        Supreme poverty is heavy
lifting, then heofenly living—as a hull enters
a berg's wake or a whale's, that spreading calm
after large passage,
its muted draw silkenly forgiving
micro-seethings across the dark total.
One follows. Yet entrance is all,
poured past stir to an ooze accuracy.
And no path leads to this domain.

∫

Brattleboro, Vermont, 1994
Roslindale, Cambridge, & Magnolia, Massachusetts, 1998
Higganum, Connecticut, 2006
& Brunswick, Maine, 2015

CONTENTS

Two

DENARIVS

squaring circles

Three
CΛELVM
marching up-country

Four

THE BEWITCHED GROOM

bucking insanity,
surviving guilt

www.ingramcontent.com/pod-product-compliance
Lightning Source LLC
Chambersburg PA
CBHW022000160426
43197CB00007B/199
* 9 7 8 1 8 4 8 6 1 4 7 3 4 *